Another wonderful, feel-good book from a writer who writes with such a great mix of warmth and humour! Her books are just the kind of escapism we need in times like these. Looking forward to seeing what Susanna brightens up our days with next!

Susanna is a wonderful story teller with a great sense of humour in her books. You're left feeling the magic in her words. I want to live in one of these wonderful villages in God's own county...Yorkshire.

Adventure, escapism, reality and a little bit of magic and mystery. Timeless, ageless and a great page turner. Give her books a try they all include this great recipe Enjoy a few days out in the brilliantly crafted stories.

Really, really enjoyed this book, kept me absorbed all the way through, would definitely recommend it and could read it again

I enjoyed reading this book. There were some things that made me laugh when reading through. It was a light hearted, warming easy read. Something that just made me smile the whole way though. An enjoyable read and I do recommend it.

I loved this follow on story and became more engaged with the wonderful characters. A really uplifting read. I do hope there are more stories to come involving the same people, there is so much more scope and stories to follow up. Please say there will be!

1

Susanna Scott lives in a seaside town on the Yorkshire Coast and enjoys reading, gardening, tap and jazz dancing and being with her family.

Also by Susanna Scott

The Gypsy Caravan
The Winterfell Stone
Weaver's Green
Acorn Cottage Christmas
and for children
Robin Hood and the Wolfshead Tree.

Susanna Scott @yorkshirecoastwriter on Facebook.

DRUID'S OAK FARM

Susanna Scott

ISBN - 9798392786374

For Barbara G., my wise writing buddy and long-time friend.

The Brave Old Oak, by Henry Fothergill Chorley

A song to the oak, the brave old oak,
Who hath ruled in the greenwood long;
Here's health and renown to his broad green crown,
And his fifty arms so strong.
There's fear in his frown when the sun goes down,
And the fire in the west fades out;
And he showeth his might on a wild midnight,
When the storms through his branches shout.

Then here's to the oak, the brave old oak,
Who stands in his pride alone;
And still flourish he, a hale green tree,
When a hundred years are gone!
In the days of old, when the Spring with cold
Had brightened his branches gray,
Through the grass at his feet crept maidens sweet,
To gather the dew of May.

Druid Groves

*... were respected by people who had a deeper
understanding of nature- and were places of celebration and
joy...*
*These groves were natural temples, places with a
powerful and peaceful atmosphere.*

Hageneder – The Spirit of Trees

CHAPTER 1

<u>The Meeting</u>

The view from the bench was magnificent, sitting as it did near the top of the cliffs. Even now, as November was drawing to a close, the sun played across the top of the waves. Not waves – just ripples really. The slight breeze would hardly blow the froth off a cappuccino today.

A few people were making their way up and down the path that ran a little way in front of the bench. They occasionally nodded at the sole occupant there, getting a dutiful smile in return.

Maeve McQuaid looked out to sea, imagining herself as the epitome of the wronged woman. Perhaps standing there, the wind blowing her pre-Raphaelite hair and waiting for her man to come home. She painted, metaphorically, the tragic expression of a Gothic heroine onto her own features. She imagined she looked like she was full of the anguish of lost love but knew it would look more like she was full of trapped wind to others.

Her expression soon changed into one of surprise and then delight as a brown and white dog launched itself at her, licking the alien expression away.

'Hello, you' she said, rubbing the dog behind the ears 'Have you come to cheer me up?'

'I'm sure he just wants a fuss making of him dear, but it amounts to the same thing.'

The voice came from behind the bench before an elderly lady, small and dainty, appeared in front of her. She had a silver-white bob, a tiny, pointed nose, crinkly eyes and a welcoming smile. She made Maeve with her five foot seven, nine stone frame, seem positively enormous, although she was sure she was just about average.

This delicate creature suddenly spoiled the illusion by turning round to reveal a backpack that would have floored Arnold Schwarzenegger in his prime. It hid her head from Maeve's sight, making her look like a turtle with a green canvas shell. She looked like she'd been backpacking in Bali on an O.A.P gap year. Maeve stared in astonishment.

'Could you give me a hand?' the woman grunted as she struggled to get out of the straps.

'Of course.'

Maeve jumped up, recovering her manners and her equilibrium at the same time. If anyone was going to interrupt her 'feeling sorry for herself' mood, this person would be interesting, at least.

'So tell me then' said her companion, now divested of her baggage and sitting next to her 'why do you need cheering up?'

'Oh it's nothing' came the standard reply but the woman was having none of it.

'I don't suppose you said it for fun, so while I rest my weary bones, you might as well tell me your problems. Just offload them to a stranger. Best way. Then I'll be off on my travels, and you'll never see me again.'

'Where are you travelling?' Maeve asked, still picturing a small, white-haired turtle dancing in a drink-fueled haze around a beach campfire in Bali.

'My question first' the woman said, turning towards her 'then my life story if you want it.'

'Well, I need cheering up for a few reasons really.'

The woman clapped her hands in anticipation and the springer spaniel jumped up in expectation.

'I just got sacked. Well, not exactly sacked. And not just. It all started a while ago really.'

The woman looked at her seriously, pinning Maeve with her eyes. After a few seconds, she said,

'Let's start here. I'm Beth Ingram. I've been on a walking holiday up part of the East Coast and I'm just on my way to Scarborough to catch the train home.' She held her hand out.

Not Bali then, thought Maeve as she shook the tiny hand, privately wondering if Yorkshire in November wasn't too cold for travelling turtles.

'I'm Maeve McQuaid.'

'Ooh, Irish name. Are you Irish? Originally? Sorry to interrupt.'

Maeve was used to this, and the long curly red hair and green eyes didn't help either.

'My parents were. They moved across to Durham though before my brother was born. He was born there, and I was born four years later in Yorkshire, so I haven't got the accent.'

'You do have an Irish inflection dear, from your parents no doubt. But please go on.'

I worked on a country estate a couple of miles away which was open to the public. At first, I helped organize events there, both in the house and in the grounds. I had lots of ideas but no one wanted to listen, they were stuck in the past. I found I preferred being outside though, so when an assistant gardener's job came up, I thought I'd try my luck and ended up on the gardening team. I think possibly because my boyfriend Kevin had worked there for a few years and put in a good word for me. I learnt a lot in a short time and I loved the job. Not long ago, Kevin finished with me because he said I was boring.'

'I'm sure that's not true,' said Beth.

'It possibly is,' replied Maeve.

'Typical victim's reply but go on, I promise I won't interrupt anymore.'

Uh-huh, thought Maeve but went on anyway.

'Things became quite awkward at work after that and in the end, I was 'made redundant,' even though I'd been on the team four years and the last person only started the year before.

'Didn't you contest it?' said the lady who wouldn't interrupt again.

'I thought about it but the redundancy money came in handy as I'd had to move out of Kevin's flat and find somewhere to live again. I heard later that he had moved a new girlfriend in there a couple of weeks after I left, so she may have been around before. I don't know and I don't care.

'All I could find was a bedsit which was the only thing I could afford, just as a stop-gap. Now, there's very little chance of me finding anywhere better to live until I find a job. That's proving harder than I imagined though, there's nothing in this town at all and I may have to move away. So' Maeve finished, 'that's my tale of woe.'

'You poor girl' said Beth, rubbing Maeve's shoulder, 'I'm sure something will come along soon.'

'I wish I were that sure but honestly, don't worry. I don't let anything get me down for long.'

'I can tell that' Beth smiled 'You have an open, cheerful-looking face, the kind whose owner always makes the best of things.'

'That's true, believe it or not. I have a million ideas buzzing around in my head about what I can do next but I like to have a good moan to myself, now and again,' Maeve grinned.

'You just need that little push in the right direction and you'll soon forget your troubles.'

'What troubles?' asked Maeve, laughing.

Beth was just what she needed at this moment and she was a great believer in fate.

'What about you? You look like you might have a story to tell?' she asked, pointing to Beth's huge rucksack.

'That backpack has been across deserts and through jungles with me. On remote islands and across the snowy wastes too. Now, it is accompanying me on walks in our own British

Isles. That's all I can afford now I'm afraid, camping and the occasional stay in a B&B. It's also all I want now. I've done everything I wanted to do and I haven't seen enough of this country as I ignored it in favour of harsher climates, which didn't do my skin any good.'

Beth laughed and pointed to her face which was indeed wrinkled but they mostly looked like laugh lines as she seemed to have a permanent smile on her face.

'Although I've possibly seen most of what I want to see here now too. Not everywhere though, not yet. I haven't done the Orkney and Shetland Isles yet and I'd like to do that before I pop my clogs.'

Maeve wondered how old she was. It was so difficult to tell as she looked fit and healthy. Mid-seventies perhaps?

'I needed this trip to get away from home for a while.'

'Why?' Maeve frowned.

'Oh, money troubles, family troubles, the usual.' She laughed, then seeing Maeve's serious face, she went on.

'I own a very old and very large house in Ryedale on the edge of the North Yorkshire Moors. It's falling to bits and there is no money coming in to repair it. I could save money by getting rid of the gardener but the grounds are extensive and I need him. Besides, he grows most of the food we eat. The girl who comes in to cook and clean is indispensable too – and she needs the money. There are no jobs to be found where I live either. They are both so good about me paying them less than the basic wage. Shh! Don't tell anyone,' she said, putting her fingers to her lips.

'The house has been in the family for so many generations but I might be the last as my great-nephew doesn't want it and couldn't afford it anyway. I'd be just handing down trouble. He's in France at the moment. I haven't got anyone else to leave it to as I never had children. I can't betray my ancestors by selling it so I suppose it will go to him when I die, whether he wants it or not. He can do what he wants with it then as I won't know about it.'

'I'd be tempted to leave it to the local dog's home' huffed Maeve indignantly.

'Don't think that hasn't crossed my mind. I do worry about the people living there now though.'

'So you're not on your own then?' asked Maeve, who had privately wondered why she needed a cook for one person.

'No, there are five of us. We're a bunch of misfits and eccentrics if the truth were told. My brother and I ran it for many years as a creative

16

retreat. My grandfather had done the same before us, so we were continuing his dream. Artists, writers, poets, craftsmen etc. We funded it then as our grandparents left us comfortably off but as the years went by, the money dwindled and people left.

'The five residents now contribute what we can – but the arts have never paid well unless you get the lucky breaks so...'

The pause lengthened.

'I thought you were supposed to be cheering me up?' smiled Maeve gently.

'Oh sorry dear but not to worry. For both of us, I mean. Things have a way of working out for the best in the end, even if it doesn't seem like it at the time.'

Maeve grinned, feeling her companion's natural enthusiasm pushing through and starting to rub off on her.

'Well' said Beth, jumping up like a twenty-year-old and grabbing her backpack once more. 'I'd better be off if I want to get to Scarborough in time. If I miss the train home, I'll have to camp out another night and I'm wanting my own bed now.'

The spaniel roused himself, shaking his ears and looking alert.

Maeve felt quite sad. She would miss this little lady and her easy, good-natured ways, even after an acquaintance of all of half an hour. After Beth had scrabbled about in one of the zip pockets for something, Maeve stood up to help her with the heavy load, securing it tightly.

'Here' said Beth, holding out a card 'this is my name and address – please come and visit if you're ever up that way.' She held out another card and a pen to Maeve. 'Put your name and address on there for me and, if I'm ever round here again, perhaps we can have lunch?'

'I'd love that' said Maeve – and meant it.

She scribbled quickly on the back of the card and handed it over. Beth leant forward to peck her on the cheek and Maeve had visions of the burden on her back tipping her up and falling on top of her, squashed under the enormous backpack. However, Beth carried it out with aplomb.

As she waved the woman and dog off, she looked at the card for the first time.

LADY ELIZABETH INGRAM
DRUID'S OAK FARM
HAWBURY
NORTH YORKSHIRE
TEL.   076970

CHAPTER 2

<u>Three months later</u>

Druid's Oak Farm,
Hawbury

Dear Maeve,
I hope this letter finds you well. Actually, I
hope this letter just finds you, especially as I'm not
sure you're still at the address you gave me. You
will still be there, I expect, if you have found
another job – but I hope you haven't.

That sounds awful when I re-read it but I have
my reasons for writing it. What I mean is, I could
really do with some help here at the farm, mostly
in the grounds. Bert is wonderful in the kitchen
gardens and at whizzing across the grass on his
sit-on mower but has had to neglect the formal
garden etc. to do so. The shrubs are mostly small

trees now for want of attention. Not his fault, there is only so much one person can do. As you have experience in gardening matters, I wondered if you could help out?

Now the hard bit. As you know, I can only afford a very basic wage but I can offer accommodation and food with the rest of us in the house, all in. Warmth too, to a certain extent.

I do hope you can take this up as I felt an affinity with you when we met and you might just be the answer to my prayers.

All my very best

Beth x

p.s. In the envelope is money for a bus ticket to Helmsley. I will pick you up from there. Just come for a visit and see what you make of us.

*

Maeve put the letter down and looked around her at the boxes. Her entire life, thrown into three large packing cases. The bedsit was spotless, the only evidence of occupation being a sleeping bag on the stripped single bed, a book on the windowsill and a kettle. All ready for when she had to vacate the place first thing in the morning.

Maeve believed in fate and after this intervention, she would believe in it forevermore. Could anything have been better timed? In twenty-four hours she would have been back at

20

her parents' house and in her own childhood room– no further on in life than she had been ten years ago.

The phone call she had to make now might be difficult but she wasn't sure that her parents wanted her presence there any more than she wanted to be there, much as they all loved each other. They had their own independent lives now. Free at last of her and her brother, they had countless hobbies, so she couldn't blame them if they wanted their newfound independence left intact. They wouldn't say anything of course but there might be a secret sigh of relief on both sides.

In the end, her mother had managed to sound sad that they wouldn't see her and relieved at the same time. With vague references to a new job, Maeve promised she would be over to see them when she could and, if she sent Harvey back with the boxes, could they store them for her until later?

Harvey was the groundsman at their golf club and was always up for earning more money on the side. He was driving here in his van for 10 a.m. tomorrow and Maeve was relieved that it was only the boxes that were going back with him now.

Scrabbling about in them, she fished out essentials that she would need and packed them into her big rucksack, still half the size of Beth's.

She filled a suitcase with clothes and boots. Humming to herself, she picked up her book and flung herself on the bed to read but she read the same paragraph four times as curiosity about her new job took over.

*

Maeve looked out of the bus windows at the unfamiliar countryside which somehow had a familiar feel. She saw signs for Helmsley Castle and Rievaulx Abbey and realised she *had* been here when she was young and her parents had taken a holiday cottage nearby for the family. She loved exploring castles, abbeys and ancient monuments as history was one of her favourite subjects as was evident by her books. She looked forward to visiting some while she was here.

She looked away now as a feeling of guilt overshadowed the pleasure. It wasn't her fault that Beth might have misunderstood, as Maeve hadn't actually said she was a trained gardener or a plant expert. She just did as she was told. Put this plant here, chop those plants down, cut those bushes back. Would four years of watching, doing and learning count as an apprenticeship? Possibly, as she had enjoyed her job and had come to recognize all the plants and trees on the estate, along with the techniques to deal with them.

She had fished out from one of the boxes - a charity shop find - an Encyclopedia of Gardening. It was now making her rucksack extra heavy as she didn't want to let Beth down and she might need it for reference.

The bus pulled into Helmsley town square and Maeve stood up, heaving her rucksack onto her shoulder, knocking the specs off the man behind her. As she turned around, he made a swift jump back out of her way, treading on the toes of the woman behind him. Feeling embarrassed, she bent to retrieve his glasses but bumped heads with him as he did the same. Mumbling a general apology with reddening cheeks, she thankfully got off the bus.

As she gazed around her, there was a shout of 'Miss McQuaid?' and a man in dusty overalls doffed his flat cap at her as she made her way towards him. He was leaning against an old white van with the name 'Samuel Dawson – Builder and Joiner' on the side.

'Lady Ingram asked me to take you to the farm. Beth, I mean. Still can't get used to calling her that,' he laughed.

'I know her as Beth, so Beth she will stay,' smiled Maeve, putting her rucksack in the back of the van, amongst all the planks of wood, black plastic buckets and worn old toolboxes. 'She seems more like a Beth, doesn't she?'

'She does, I'll agree. While we're at it,' and he pointed at the signwriting 'Please call me Sam, not Samuel.'

'Only if you call me Maeve and not Miss McQuaid.'

They both laughed and got in the van, setting off North of Helmsley on a winding narrow road climbing slowly upwards.

Sam kept a running commentary going about his son, Billy, who worked with him now and would be having his name on the van but at the moment, he was spending most of his time doing odd jobs up at the farm. He also said he was Carole's dad too but as it was assumed she would know who that was, she didn't like to ask. He then pointed out various houses that he'd been working on just past Helmsley until the houses thinned out and the glorious countryside opened up.

It was a cold, crisp February with a bright sun shining down over the hills, highlighting the tops of trees and casting shadows below them. Wooded areas were dotted all over and rising above that was a flat-topped hill, forming a backdrop to the dale that dipped below it. Houses seem very scarce round here, thought Maeve after about five minutes, just as Sam took a steep left-hand bend and a small village appeared magically in front of her.

'This is Hawbury village, where I live. There's a general shop where you can buy most essential things but if you wanted specific things, you'd have to go back to Helmsley. There is a pub though,' he laughed, nodding in the direction of The Falcon, perched – so to speak – on the edge of the village. Maeve thought it probably had some of the most spectacular views of any beer garden in Ryedale. It may have been a climb to get here but the views were the upside. Sam continued past the pub and over to the left.

After a short, snaking climb through one of the wooded areas, the land suddenly formed into a plateau below the hill. The van carried on for another mile or so across gently undulating pasture with the occasional hawthorn hedge dividing the land. There wasn't a house anywhere as far as she could see.

'Nearly there,' Sam said and Maeve leaned forward, peering through the windscreen. No, still nothing. Then, as they rounded another stand of trees and negotiated a dip in the road, it was there in front of them. Druid's Oak Farm.

They drove up to the iron gates, propped open permanently by the look of things and as they crunched along on the long gravel driveway, she caught sight of huge kitchen gardens through an open gateway in a brick wall. When she looked to her right in front of the house, there was a vast expanse of lawn leading down to a wooded area. In the middle of the lawn stood a large and ancient oak. Sam pulled up in front of the great wooden door of the farm and Maeve got out.

This isn't a farm, whatever it's called, she thought, it's an Elizabethan Hall. It was a Tudor black and white building, the black beams at right angles and diagonals, not following any particular pattern. The white paint or plaster was flaking and the beams were more faded grey than black. The windows were leaded with small panes-within-panes. The thatch hung down from the roof and had an attractive scalloped ridge at the apex of the roof. The thatch was more green than grey with moss and even grass growing up there. At either end, someone had built matching annexes, presumably at a later period, as the windows facing the front looked more Georgian and the thatch on the roof was without the scalloped ridge. It was desperately in need of TLC but Maeve fell in love with it on sight.

'Maeve!' came a shout from the now open door 'I can't tell you how pleased I am to see you.'

Maeve beamed with pleasure as Beth ran down the steps to give her a hug with a happy Springer spaniel at her heels.

CHAPTER 3

'So, are you here for a visit or are you taking the job?'

Maeve was sitting opposite Beth in front of a log fire. It was set in a battered old iron stove which had seen better days. She held a mug of tea in her hands which proclaimed, 'Art is a lie that makes us realise truth' and Beth had obviously progressed from the small talk. Maeve replied to her question in like manner.

'I have to be honest with you, I have no job and was just about to leave my bedsit and move back to my parents' house. So, if it's okay with you, I'd like to accept the job offer. Although in the same spirit of honesty, it's not just the job, now I've seen the place, I'm looking forward to working in these surroundings.'

There was a pause.

'And possibly taking honesty *too* far, I have no gardening qualifications whatsoever and just four years of gardening experience to call on' she finished quietly.

'Experience is what we need and, more than that, we need someone who is enthusiastic about what they are doing and will hopefully love this place as much as we do.'

Maeve smiled and reached for the piece of Victoria sponge on the small table at her side.

'I think I love it already. Where is everyone by the way?' she added as an afterthought. Five of them lived there, Beth had said.

'Oh, round and about. They each have their own study, studio or workshop as well as their bedrooms. I sometimes only see them here in the kitchen. It's the only room we all congregate in for our breakfasts and for our meal in the evening. It's the only thing I insist on. No good having a community that doesn't commune together occasionally. Some of the others tend not to be very sociable, they like to be alone, as do a lot of people involved in the arts or creative industries.'

Beth reflected on this for a moment then jumped up.

'Grab your rucksack and let me show you where you're sleeping. Then I'll give you a tour of the house. I'll leave it up to Bert to give you a tour of the grounds.'

As they headed to the door, a plump young woman, apple-cheeked and cheery, bustled in. Her hair was as curly as Maeve's own but was just touching her shoulders and obviously dyed blonde, judging by the black stripe down the parting.

'Did you ask your dad about the leak in my bedroom?' Beth asked her.

'Yes' was the short reply.

'What did he say?'

'He just handed me a bucket from his van and said, "Here's the sticking plaster for the symptom and when it's eventually re-thatched, we can cure the cause."' The girl grinned.

'Yes, he would,' Beth sighed but a smile played around her lips. 'I won't have to trouble him for a bucket, there's already one there in situ. Just pray we don't get any downpours as a new thatch is a long way off.'

'We'll get there' the girl said kindly.

'Are you Sam's daughter then?' Maeve asked, recognizing the bucket reference 'Carole, wasn't it?'

'I am – and you must be Maeve. I can tell by the Irish accent. Are you staying with us now?'

'Yes, I am,' answered Maeve, wondering again at the mention of an Irish accent she didn't think she had.

'That's good,' said Carole, collecting the mugs and plates, and taking them over to the old pot Belfast sink. 'We all hoped you would.'

Maeve was glad she was staying as she would have felt terrible letting everyone down if she'd hated the place on sight.

As Beth led her up the stunning oak central staircase, Maeve asked if Carole was one of the five.

'No, although I've asked her to stay as it would be easier for her than travelling to and from Hawbury every day. She's our cook and housekeeper. She's come in to cook a special dinner in your honour – but it won't be anything fancy. We eat the produce in the garden mostly so if you don't like vegetables, you'll probably starve here.'

'I do like veg and I haven't had a meal since seven this morning and that was a cereal bar, so I'll probably eat whatever you put in front of me – including the plate.'

Beth laughed and turned left at the top of the stairs.

'Your room faces the back. East, so you'll get the sun in the morning.'

She led her into a huge room with a small double stuck in the middle of it, looking lost. It had an old Candlewick bedspread on it, topped with an old-fashioned feather quilt patterned with paisley swirls. Everything looked old and worn but spotlessly clean, she could even smell the fresh smell of wash powder.

There was a single wooden wardrobe against one wall and next to the bed was a wooden bedside cabinet with a lamp on it. The smell of beeswax polish now came up to greet her as she examined the cabinet. A rag rug was on one side of the bed on top of a faded Axminster carpet. That was it really.

There was another door in the wall to her right and Beth led her through to a much smaller room. The only furniture there being a table against the opposite wall with a chair tucked under it. The threadbare carpet continued through there.

Maeve leaned forward to look out of the window and saw that she had a perfect view of the formal garden. This then, was where she would mostly be working. It was neglected and overgrown, that much was obvious, but it had good bones.

Maeve realised that neither of them had said a word since they'd come in when she heard Beth's hesitant voice.

'Is it alright? It's a bit spartan I know but maybe you can add to it over time?'

'Yes, I love it. I can see in my mind's eye how I want this and–' she wondered if this was a bit forward 'would you mind if I swapped the rooms around? Put the bed here in this small room and in the bigger room, I could get a sofa and a bookcase, then I could bring the table through and put it under the large window overlooking the garden?'

Beth watched Maeve's enthusiastic expression and breathed a sigh of relief.

'I can't tell you how happy that makes me. I was right, you obviously have creative vision which, quite frankly, is a good job in this place.'

'But it's beautiful,' said Maeve with feeling and got a heartfelt hug from Beth in return.

*

The rest of the tour was short as Beth didn't want to intrude on the inner sanctums of the others.

'We respect other people's privacy as much as we can.'

There was a bathroom across from Maeve's room and next door to someone called Glenys, which she and Glenys would share. Glenys was a poet apparently. There was a separate toilet too, par for the course in older buildings. The plumbing looked ancient and was making strange tapping noises.

The ceilings were all quite low in the passageway and it was a little dark, the only natural light coming from a window in a long, set back section at the top of the stairs, which Maeve noticed had bookshelves at each side and a window seat at the end.

At the far end of this side of the stairs were, Beth's 'quarters' which she happily showed her around. She took her through to a light living room at the front of the house, overlooking the large lawn and oak tree. There were sizeable, long windows to the front and side in a Georgian style and Maeve realised she was in one of the built-on extensions from a later era. At the other end was a slightly smaller room, used as a bedroom, one window overlooking the gravel path leading to the kitchen gardens and the other with the same view as Maeve. In the middle of the rooms was a bathroom, which she actually apologised for.

'Bit of a luxury, I know.'

'It's your house, Beth,' Maeve had to remind her sternly.

At the top of the stairs again, Beth gestured towards the other side, which seemed to be a mirror image of the one they'd come from.

'Tim's rooms overlooking the front. He's a woodworker.' Maeve wanted to ask questions about this, but Beth went on.

'And at the far end is Michael, an artist, who has the same set of rooms as I do. There are spare rooms down there too, but I thought you'd rather be on the women's side, especially bathroom-wise' she smiled.

Very true, thought Maeve, she didn't fancy trotting across to the bathroom in the morning in her fluffy jimjams, to be confronted by a pair of hairy strangers.

'Oh dear,' said Beth, looking out of the landing window, 'it's started raining.'

Maeve turned in time to see and hear the rain suddenly battering against the glass.

'I think we'd better call off your tour of the garden for now. I think I might give Carole a hand now so why don't you have a wander around downstairs and see where everything is? Then, fingers crossed, there should be enough hot water if you want a bath. Just come down to the kitchen when you're ready, we eat at 6.30 p.m.'

Beth curved down to the right at the bottom of the stairs towards the kitchen while Maeve made for the door to the right of the entrance.

CHAPTER 4

Beth noticed the pile of potatoes that Carole had started on and picked up a small kitchen knife to help her.

'Do you think she'll stay?' asked Carole, looking up with a frown.

'Do you know, I believe she will. What with Phillip deserting us the Christmas before last, and Fliss just after Spring that same year, I felt like we were dwindling away to nothing. What had felt like a family, was slowly disintegrating. My 'children' were all flying the nest.

'Maeve though – she seemed to have an immediate affinity with the place. She said she loved it. She is too guileless to say it if she doesn't mean it. I don't think there is an insincere bone in her body.'

'That's your bugbear isn't it – insincerity?'

'It is I'm afraid. I'd rather someone came out with the truth, even if it's harder to take than tell lies with a smile on their face, for their own ends.'

'But you think she loves it? Has she met everyone yet?' asked Carole, with a meaningful stare.

'No one. She'll have that pleasure at dinner. Why?' smiled Beth, 'do you think it will put her off?'

'It might make her think twice,' answered Carole who most definitely 'came out with the truth'.

Beth chuckled to herself and thought of the small community that was left here.

Glenys could be abrasive and defensive. They all seemed to offend her on a daily basis without knowing exactly why. She had been here the longest of the people left here, she was around sixty, and Beth was very fond of her. She thought Glenys might be fond of her too, but it was very hard to judge. She did feel sorry for Glenys but never in a million years would she let her know that.

Glenys felt like she had to contribute something to the creative community and started writing poetry and occasional 'stream-of-consciousness' prose, like a latter-day Virginia Woolf. Both were mediocre at best. Beth didn't like to admit it, even to herself but there was no getting away from it.

Glenys had been an English mistress at an independent girl's school, where the pupils had reduced her to a gibbering wreck over something personal. Not totally their fault, she had told Beth, as their teacher was overworked and teetering on the edge of a precipice where, at any time, a harsh word, a practical joke or even a black look could have brought her tumbling down. The doctor told her she would have a nervous breakdown if she didn't take time off and rest.

She had come to Druid's Oak Farm over twelve years ago now for peace and quiet to get over it. She had stayed on, unable to face a return to her earlier life.

Beth put the peeled potatoes in the large pan of water bubbling away on the hotplate of the iron stove. The stove was ancient but still did its job perfectly.

'Are they really all that scary?' she asked Carole, going back to earlier.

'I'm used to them now but they might seem a bit odd to a newcomer, don't you think? Tim's okay I suppose. Doesn't say much to anyone though – even me.'

Carole picked up a cauliflower abstractedly and cut off the stalk with more force than was needed.

Beth took all this in. It was well known that Carole had a 'thing' for Tim. Well known to everyone but Tim, it seemed. Beth thought that Tim was remaining ignorant on purpose. Carole was a lovely girl and they would make a good couple, but Tim would have to get over his chronic shyness first.

The reason he had come here was because it was fairly remote and he wouldn't have to deal with people en masse. He could get on with his heritage crafts in splendid isolation in one of the wooden barns. She knew that mealtimes were an ordeal for him but she still insisted he was there, for his own sake. He would never overcome his unsociability without human contact.

He became quite defensive when Carole tried to jolly him along, taking cups of tea and some cake to him at the barn, at every given opportunity. Whether he realised it or not, it had already done him good. He was much better than when he first came here.

'I hope she likes plain cooking,' Carole said, breaking into Beth's thoughts. 'I don't do any fancy stuff.'

'I'm sure she will. She doesn't seem the type to worry about what food she eats. She's just like us, she'll fit in well. Besides, your cooking is delicious, plain or not. Now, what else can I do?'

This seemed to mollify Carole who gave Beth a grateful smile.

'You can start peeling the apples.'

Beth reached for the apples, all individually wrapped in tissue paper from where they had been stored in the larder. Her thoughts ran on again.

Michael, of course, was an enigma. Not one of the scary ones at all, she didn't think, although he sometimes appeared remote to other people, even unfriendly at times. She personally put this down to his artistic nature, getting lost in his work to the exclusion of everyone and everything else. His paintings really were quite wonderful.

He did have a good side though. He was practical and could be kind when he wanted to be. He also had a sense of humour, something that was sadly lacking in Glenys and Tim, although theirs could be lurking beneath the surface, there was always hope. Thinking about it, Michael's humour could be sarcastic and could be mistaken for rudeness by those who didn't know him well. She knew some people found him hard to deal with but, well, she had a soft spot for him.

And then there was Ruadhan. Beth smiled, as everyone did when they thought of Ruadhan.

Suddenly, with a shock of blustery rain, the back door banged open, admitting the only family member she hadn't thought of – Rusty.

'Aw Billy,' shouted Carole, 'what did you bring that wet dog in here for? Look! Muddy pawprints all over the floor.'

'He was whining to come out of the workshop. Bert said to bring him over to get warm.' Billy addressed his sister in an aggrieved tone.

As if to prove him right, Rusty shook his coat all over the now muddy stone tiles and made straight for his place in front of the oven. He gave Carole a supercilious look as he passed her. Beth smiled; she was sure he could understand everything they said.

Carole came over and bent down to him.

'How am I supposed to get dinner ready with you in my way and muddy prints to clean up?' she asked Rusty, who knowing she didn't *really* mean it, reached up to lick her nose, wagging his tail at the same time. Carole stroked behind his ears, which he loved. She straightened up.

'Now look!' She held up her wet hands. 'I'm going to have to wash them now.'

'I didn't make you stroke him,' laughed Billy.

41

'Is dad coming up for you?'

'Yes, about six-ish, after he's finished work. Are you wanting a lift home?

'In this weather? Course I am.'

'Oh' interrupted Beth, 'I thought you were staying to dinner with us today Carole.'

'I would have normally, but cycling or even freewheeling, a mile and a half in the dark in this deluge isn't something I fancy.'

She looked disappointed, even so. She could have been sitting next to Tim.

'Never mind' said Beth, 'next time perhaps?'

CHAPTER 5

The room Maeve first entered took her by surprise. It was a spacious room, far bigger than she thought Elizabethan dimensions allowed for. Two long, low windows with small leaded squares let an unexpected amount of light in, despite the rain beating against them. Even so, she turned on a couple of the lamps and they threw a cosy light on the room. Window seats ran along their length, to sit and read on perhaps, or to just admire the view when you could actually see out of the window.

The ceiling was beamed but higher than the upper floor ceilings were. No one would have to duck. On her right, on the opposite wall to the windows was a magnificent fireplace. It had a wooden carved surround with an inner construction of marble-like stone. A large dog grate, piled with logs, lay inside the cavernous hearth, waiting to be lit.

Light oak panelling lined the walls and two built-in bookcases on the end wall had a door between them. Between the windows, a marble bust of a woman stood on a console table. On closer inspection, it was a very delicately formed likeness of a young Beth. On the heavy wood and glass coffee table in front of the fireplace, stood a glass vase of yellow tulips.

In the middle of the room were two brown leather three-seater sofas, at right angles to each other and a matching chair at the right of the hearth.

She crossed the old, mellow wooden floor and could now see that the sofas had lost their bounce and had caved in a little. The curtains were faded at the window edges, the rug under the coffee table was threadbare in places and some of the lead was missing in the windows. The wind was whistling down the chimney, making the room icy cold. The room somehow still felt cosy though to Maeve, as she imagined it with the fire lit in the grate. Faded splendour perhaps but a lived-in room which felt welcoming.

Opening the door at the end, she found another, much lighter room. On a sunny day, it would have light pouring in through the Georgian windows, which had larger square window panes. This must be one of the later additions tacked on the side of the main house, with Beth's rooms above it. The long wall opposite was almost floor-to-ceiling windows and perhaps would have been used as a garden room. The carpet, which was struggling to be white, covered the whole floor and a few chairs were pushed back towards the windows.

A strange room, thought Maeve, she couldn't guess its purpose but it exuded an aura of peace. It sounded fanciful but Maeve hadn't felt as peaceful and calm as she felt in this house for a long time. Beth had a lot to do with that, she thought.

Back through the sitting room into the hall, she saw the same light oak panelling lined the walls with the addition of a decorative frieze at shoulder height. Above this, next to the ornate plaster ceiling, ran a deeper and more elaborate frieze with figures and carved animals in relief. The central wooden staircase led up to the first floor and on the ground floor, to the left of the stairs, down a short passage, was the door to the kitchen that seemed to run along most of the back of the house.

On the other side of the hall were two doors. Through the right-hand door was a study or library. One wall was lined with bookshelves behind glass doors. A desk stood under one window and a small square table under the other. Two easy chairs made up the rest of the furniture.

The second door led to a narrow dining room furnished solely by a long dark, wooden table with ornately carved chairs set around it. The room, though clean and smelling of beeswax polish, had an abandoned air to it – damp and very cold. Maeve expected that they always ate in the kitchen where at least they would be warm. At the far end of the left wall, there was a door and, as she approached it, the clatter of pans and the murmur of female voices announced it as another entrance to the kitchen. There was another door in the far wall and she opened the door, realising at once it was the twin of the white-ish carpeted garden room at the other end. The floor here, however, was covered in tiles, mostly white but with smaller black diamond-shaped tiles set at intervals.

As she raised her eyes from the floor, she realised she was not alone. With a jolt, she saw there was a tall slim figure, standing silhouetted against the window, his arm raised towards a canvas in front of him.

Her cheeks reddening, she took in the face that had turned towards her in muted surprise. Brown eyes, seeming strangely green in the reflected light, very dark brown hair falling almost to his shoulders, black eyebrows, one raised in query and an amused smile playing on his lips. He had tight, paint-stained buckskin trousers on, clinging to his thighs. A vision of Robin of Sherwood, sword in hand, jumped briefly into her mind, unbidden. She lifted her eyes quickly and came to at last.

'Hello?' His deep voice came out as a question rather than a welcome.

'Oh dear, I'm so sorry. I know that Beth said not to intrude on people's privacy and I just have. I didn't realise this was your room. Studio?'

She started to back out like a Victorian servant would from her master until she saw his face relax and a wide smile appear.

'Ah, you must be the girl Beth invited, Irish by the sound of it? I'm Michael'

'Yes, I'm Maeve and I'm not Irish. I'll just go now' she whispered.

'Okay. See you at dinner, probably.'

He obviously didn't intend to stop her, so she made a hasty exit, shutting the door behind her. He was possibly mid-masterpiece and she had disturbed his concentration. Even in the middle of her embarrassment and confusion, she had to admit that most of it was caused by the fact that he was bloody gorgeous!

CHAPTER 6

Bags unpacked, quick hand-held shower in the cold bathroom, change of clothes into something a little more presentable and Maeve was on her way down to dinner. It felt like it might be a formal dinner but in a nice warm kitchen instead of a cheerless dining room.

As she entered the kitchen, she was pleased to see that Beth had changed her jumper for another similar one, so Maeve's soft, black cowl-necked jumper and black trousers weren't too dressed down. She only owned one posh frock which was now in a box in her parents' spare room.

There was a clattering sound and Carole shot out of the cloakroom with her coat pulled tightly around her.

'Have to go, dad's here. Nice to meet you Maeve' she shouted over her shoulder.

'And you…' replied Maeve to a closed door.

Another woman was standing at the oven, stirring the contents of a pan.

'Maeve, may I introduce you to Glenys, our resident poet and a good friend of mine.'

Maeve started to walk over to her with her hand held out but Glenys merely looked up mid-stir and gave her a very sour look.

'How do you do?' she said in a voice far plummier than Beth's, then carried on stirring.

'There's cutlery in that drawer if you would set the table?' asked Beth, putting a couple of heatproof table mats in the middle of the sturdy pine table.

It was pitch black outside, the raindrops on the windows reflected the warm lights inside. As she worked her way around the table, Maeve furtively glanced at Glenys. She had rather a long face, a long nose and thin lips. Her hair was very short and stuck out slightly at each side where her spectacles sat, their gold chains hanging down at either side. Her clothes, a grey blouse and cardigan, and a black skirt were very 'sensible.' How old was she? Not as old as she was making herself look, thought Maeve.

The door from the hallway opened and a young man slid in. There was no other way to describe it. It was as if he were trying to go unnoticed.

'I'm Maeve McQuaid' she said with a bright smile and held her hand out a second time. For the second time, it was rejected, as he put his head down and muttered what could have been 'Tim.'

She gave Beth a quizzical look but Beth just smiled benignly.

'Just Michael now' she said, her tiny frame carrying a large heavy-looking dish over to the table in oven-gloved hands.

'Can I help?' asked Maeve.

'Yes, there's some Pinot Grigio in the fridge if you can open it for us. You won't need a corkscrew as it's a screw-top supermarket special but at least it's alcoholic.'

'I wouldn't know what wines tasted like that *weren't* bought in a supermarket, so I can't compare it unfavourably.' Maeve laughed and was rewarded with a genuinely grateful smile that had nothing to do with the wine. Smiles were thin on the ground at the moment and dinner was going to be hard going if their two companions didn't brighten up.

Glenys brought dishes of cabbage and Brussels sprouts, while Beth brought carrots and turnip. She went back and poured gravy into two jugs and set them down on the table. They had all taken their places when Michael wandered in.

Maeve's heart gave an uncomfortable lurch at the sight of him.

'You just made it,' said Beth, trying to look stern.

'I got caught up in my work,' he said unapologetically.

'I can see that.' Beth looked pointedly at his hands, covered in two or three paint colours.

'They are *clean*,' he emphasised with a laugh. 'I didn't want to smell of white spirit where there was food, so I just used soap and water.'

He was just taking his seat when he saw Maeve.

'Ah, the amazing, blushing, Irish redhead! How do you do again?' He held his hand towards her and they shook hands.

So, he had noticed her blushing earlier and she could feel her cheeks burning again. At least he was friendly – and smiled. Although she did mumble 'not Irish' under her breath.

'I think it's the red hair that makes everyone think I'm Irish,' she said as he turned to give her a bemused look.

'Mm. If you say so' he replied and then leant forward to pick up a serving spoon until Beth tapped the back of his hand.

'Ah – ah!' she admonished and put her hands together.

They all began to say 'For what we are about to receive, may the Lord make us truly thankful. Amen.'

As Michael dived for the spoon again, Maeve realise how surprised she was at hearing grace offered before a meal. She couldn't think why unless it was because she thought of Beth as a free spirit and not religious. Perhaps she wasn't, it might have been a habit that they continued from years ago. She couldn't remember hearing it said at a table since her schooldays and that had been abandoned before she left. She must join in the next time. She wasn't religious but wasn't militant about it and was happy to fit in. She became aware of Beth telling Michael off once more.

'Our newest member of the family first, Michael,' she said, trying to stop him before he deposited a large helping on his plate. Too late. Beth sighed.

'Ah, second then?' he smiled, handing her the spoon.

She dug into the dish of shepherd's pie – good warming food was appreciated on a night like this. She mentally counted up the people around the table. She was starving but she didn't want to take more than her share.

Five people, counting herself, she thought as she tucked into the generous plateful. When they first met, Beth had said there were five of them. Someone was missing.

'Did you say there were five people living here before I came?' Maeve asked Beth.

'Yes, it doesn't look like Rowan's remembered. Perhaps tomorrow?'

Everyone smiled fondly at this statement, even Glenys and Tim. This Rowan, whoever he or she was, must be a miracle worker. She frowned, was it Rowan? It sounded more like Ruan - but before she could ask, Beth said,

'So, you've already met?' Beth glanced between Maeve and Michael.

'We met earlier. In my studio. Briefly.'

'In your studio?' Beth looked concerned. 'I forgot to tell her to keep away from you when you were working in case you scared her off.'

'I was perfectly pleasant, wasn't I, Maeve McQuaid?'

'He was actually.' Maeve addressed Beth.

'Of course, I was only daubing the background and not any more intricate details or I'd have turned into a warty green ogre, chased you out of the door then felled you with my foul, swamp-like breath.'

'There are tablets you can take for that now' remarked Maeve, without missing a beat.

There was a moment of surprise travelling around the table then both Beth and Michael burst out laughing.

'She answers back!' said Michael incredulously.

'She does when pushed' replied Maeve and a gleeful smile passed between them.

CHAPTER 7

Maeve had the kitchen to herself for now. They had all finished breakfast without being honoured by Michael's presence – or the elusive Rowan's – and Beth had gone to her meditation room to practice yoga for a while. This was the garden room at the other end of the house from Michael's studio. She remembered feeling calm and peaceful while she was in there and, knowing its purpose now, she realised why.

Beth had explained over breakfast that when the house was full in the earlier years of the community, she had taught yoga and meditation and practised Reiki. Now, she went on, anyone who wanted to could join her in the room at 7 a.m. for alternate sessions of meditation and yoga. Maeve preferred to do her own version of meditation outside amongst trees, flowers, water and fresh air, where she found her own kind of peace. Yoga, however, she might have a go at, as she would have to keep supple with the hard work she had planned in the garden.

She poured a second cup of coffee and checked out her surroundings in more depth. Beams ran along the length of the kitchen, beams of course being a given in a building like this. They were a bleached oak colour apart from over the black range oven which looked as though it had sent a few stray flames in their direction over the years.

Un-curtained windows looked over the formal garden. The light flowed in from the East through the leaded windows, especially today as the sun had decided to come out.

The white plaster on the walls was divided by thin wooden beams. Panelling in here would have been too much of a fire risk perhaps? Two settles were pushed against the walls and both had bright, jungle-style seating cushions, reminiscent of the turn-of-the-century paintings of Henri Rousseau. Were they the work of an earlier resident?

Two wooden carver chairs at either side of the range had cushions of the same bright material and a large dog basket was laid between one chair and the warmth of the oven. Its owner now came flying in to take his place there, for all of three seconds, before he ran off to guide Beth, who had just entered, back to her chair. Carole followed her and went over to the sink. Rusty then padded across to Maeve, putting his paws on her knees and gazing at her imploringly.

'Hello, Rusty. Do you want a walk?' she made the mistake of saying as she tickled under his chin.

The chorus of 'Shh' from the two women coincided with a high-pitched, excited whimper from Rusty as he ran around in circles. He stopped after every rotation to stare at her expectantly.

The hall door opened and, seeing the dog's antics, Michael shook his head.

'Who said the forbidden word?' he chided.

'I did, I'm afraid' answered Maeve, putting her hand tentatively in the air like a small schoolgirl.

'We'll forgive you. You didn't know any better, my child. Ah, coffee' he said, getting a clean mug from the drainer.

'What about breakfast? We didn't see you earlier and you must be hungry?' asked Beth.

'I'll just make a slice of toast.'

'It's no wonder you're so skinny,' said Carole.

'Skinny? My dear Carole, I have muscles – see?'

He put his arms up to the side like a circus strongman, to show off an impressive display of biceps. Maeve sighed inwardly.

'I think the words you are looking for are slim and toned,' he grinned. 'You could add ridiculously good-looking to those if you had a mind to.'

'I don't,' Carole replied, deadpan.

'Do you know your way around the house now Maeve?' said Beth, ignoring the macho display.

'I do – and it really is beautiful.'

'If cold,' added Michael.

'But it won't be in Summer' replied Maeve, then after a moment's thought, she turned back to Beth.

'You know Beth, I don't understand why your nephew doesn't want to inherit this place. He must be mad. I know it needs things doing to it but it would make him a wonderful home in gorgeous surroundings. Does he say why he doesn't want it?'

Vaguely, Maeve was aware of Carole making a lot of coughing noises over the sink. Beth just smiled her serene smile without answering. The answer came from an unexpected source.

'Because he would end up like his great-aunt, slowly but steadily heading towards bankruptcy. If there was any way we could stop it from falling down without the need for money, then I would jump at the chance of owning it. Apart from the fact that would mean Beth had departed this life. I'm trying not to think about it all.'

Michael took a sip of his coffee and sat back, enjoying the effect his revelation had on Maeve. When she had managed to close her mouth after taking her foot out of it and begin breathing again, she said softly,

'Have you got a shovel?'

'Why?' asked Michael. 'You've already dug the hole.'

'Well, I thought that if I dig a bit deeper, we might reach a layer of sand and then you could stick your head in it, like an ostrich.'

It was Carole's turn to stand open-mouthed now.

'I know the problem is there,' Michael explained, but while I can't do anything about it, it's pointless getting stressed over it.'

'Then *think* of something to do! This house deserves that, as well as your aunt don't you think? If we all put our heads together, including – and especially – you, then we might be able to save it.'

'I want to cheer,' said Beth.

'So do I,' said Carole.

'Bloody hell. You really do speak your mind, don't you?' said Michael, with a grin that reached his genuinely amused eyes.

Maeve suddenly realised she had been here less than twenty-four hours and she was already berating the heir.

'I'm going to put my boots on,' she mumbled and headed to the cloakroom.

After she'd gone, Michael said quietly to his aunt,

'Well, she'll certainly liven the place up. She's wasted as a gardener; she should be on a soapbox as a politician.'

'Far too honest,' replied his aunt, 'besides, gardening was only part of the reason I wanted her to come here.'

'Go on?'

'She helped organise events at a small stately home a few years ago. I had a feeling she might have some ideas of how to save this place – and it looks like I was right.'

'Crafty as ever' Michael smiled.

'Although, even if she didn't do anything but live here, I'm glad she came. Now, Rusty's been waiting patiently, poor chap. While you're taking him out, you can show Maeve around the grounds.'

Michael winced.

'Do you think I'll make it back alive?' he asked.

CHAPTER 8

Things still felt a little awkward for Maeve as she tried to keep pace with Michael's long strides across the grass. Rusty bounded along in front of them, occasionally stopping to make sure they were still there. They neared the Druid's Oak and Maeve cleared her throat.

'Why is it called the Druid's Oak?'

'That's something you'll have to ask Rowan,' he replied, not breaking stride.

She ran a few steps.

'Why didn't she tell me you were her nephew – or grand-nephew?

He seemed to take pity on her and slowed down to face her.

'I don't call her great-aunt – or even aunt, she's just Beth. And it probably didn't even occur to her as half the time she's on another spiritual planet. Yet...the other half she's so sharp she could cut herself. A bit like you really.'

'Like me?'

'Yes, you're an unusual mix of innocence, intelligence – and verbal violence.'

They caught each other's eye and started to laugh, which eased the tension, prompting Maeve to apologise.

'I'm so sorry. The words just tumble out. My ex said I was too honest for my own good.'

'I can see why my aunt took to you. She holds honesty in high regard as long as it's not too cruel. For the record, so do I. You were right about avoiding the subject of the inheritance. Although I genuinely don't want my aunt to die and that's what inheritance would mean – but I do have a lazy mind anyway.'

'I should have been kinder though because it does seem an enormous task. Billy was trying to repair a rotting door frame earlier, but as I said, if we all put our heads together, something might come out of it.'

He smiled.

'You've seen us all; we haven't got an ounce of get up and go between us. Even Beth is too laid back – or she might even be joining me in sticking our heads in the sand. If anyone can rally us though, it will be you. A breath of fresh air.'

Maeve thought privately that the only thing that would get Tim or Glenys to join in and help, would be firecrackers up their...

'I should have started with the formal garden really,' said Michael, breaking into her thoughts. 'as that's where you'll mostly be working.'

They were at the left of the grounds, skirting the edge of the wood which continued down to the tree line at the bottom.

'There's nothing much here, garden-wise, that will need your attention but you might as well get an idea of the geography of the place.'

They were nearing the trees at the lower end of the grounds, the farm quite a way behind them now. Yet another area of woodland, thought Maeve, or maybe it just continued all the way around. They plunged into the wood and spent a few minutes negotiating a variety of deciduous trees, all bare of leaves and only recognisable now by their shape or their bark. Maeve could see oak, ash, beech, birch and sycamore. Rusty was leading the way, occasionally getting side-tracked by insects in rotting wood stumps or fungi, which he sniffed guardedly and which made him sneeze all over them.

She was just trying to identify what could have been a horse-chestnut tree when she noticed the light quality was changing. She could make out a clearing ahead and, as they walked through a neat line of elegant silver birches, she could see that these trees almost met up in a circle, enclosing the clearing as if protecting it.

At the far end, there was a gap in the circle and through it, she could glimpse a natural pool. Behind that was a ten-foot wall of boulders, forming a natural rock garden with ferns growing amongst them. The rocks formed the background to the small waterfall or cascade now running into the pool. Rusty started to run happily towards it but she could hear Michael's voice calling him back.

'No, not yet Rusty.'

Michael held back as she stepped into the clearing. She turned in a slow circle, looking up at the tall birches surrounding it, their slim branches reaching gracefully for the sky. Her eyes came down to the ground, a mixture of grass, chamomile and moss. It was surprisingly lush. The whole place just made her want to stay and drink in the atmosphere. She was reminded of the tales of fairy glades and fairy rings as she saw a circle of toadstools in the middle of the grass. What was it now? The good folklore story was that it was a sign there was a fairy village underground there. The bad story was that, if you stepped into a fairy ring, you would become invisible or fall asleep for a thousand years. She smiled at the thought. Michael laughed as he joined her.

'Yes, it has that effect on you, doesn't it? There are myths associated with this place but I'm not the one to tell them.'

Maeve looked quizzically at him but nothing more about that was forthcoming.

'Follow me,' he said, like Oberon, the faerie king, enticing her away.

They headed up to the left and after a gently sloping climb, came to the far edge of the wood. Michael pointed to a mound around ten feet wide and maybe four or five feet high. Behind it, the land changed to wild moorland.

'A bronze age burial mound, almost on the boundary of our land.'

Maeve noticed he had said *our* land as though he were now claiming possession. There was hope yet.

'It's called Winterside Howe, after Winterside Hill behind it, the flat-topped hill. If you want to know the history, you'll have to get the story from …'

'Rowan,' they both said together then laughed.

'Who is this Rowan? They've got an awful lot of stories to tell me when they eventually appear.'

'You'll find out,' he said infuriatingly, 'tonight, at dinner.'

They'd walked towards the glade and pool again and now, they were nearer to the water. Ripples appeared across the surface in perfect circles from the water falling from the rocks. Rusty was panting now, eyes darting excitedly between Michael and the pool, in anticipation.

'It's a natural spring, rising just beyond here at the top of the rocks, then running underground over to your right and emerging into Hawbury Beck. Then it joins the River Rye which flows through Helmsley.' He paused.

'Do you fancy a swim?' he continued. 'Rusty and I have a dip as often as we can.

Rusty heard his name and he obviously wasn't going to wait any longer. He plunged happily into the water, doggy-paddling with an ecstatic look on his face. Maeve frowned.

'Have you brought your swimming things – or a towel?' He wasn't carrying a bag.

'Don't need them,' he said as he took off his jacket and Aran sweater to reveal a breathtakingly buff body. He slowly started undoing the zip of his jeans.

'No! I mean – I'm too – too cold to swim. Thank you all the same. I'm just going to…' and she strode off through to the right of the clearing and into another part of the wood, her face glowing like a beacon. She could hear him laughing and she scowled horribly while mentally sending the death stare back to him.

CHAPTER 9

Feeling flustered and annoyed with herself, Maeve kept her head down and therefore the brick-built tower looming up in front of her came as a surprise. It was hidden amongst the trees and looked like it was an abandoned folly, or perhaps some sort of store. Too far from the farm to be an icehouse perhaps but it could have been a handy log store in the woods.

The old wooden door with wrought iron hinges stood slightly ajar so she felt justified in having a quick peek. It was probably dangerously derelict inside and she ought to wear a safety hat but if she just popped her head around...

The door opened suddenly and both Maeve and the stranger jumped back in shock.

The man was about the same height as her with wild, red hair and glassy blue eyes. He stared closely at her as if he was missing his spectacles.

Then his face broke out into a wide beam which spread over his face in apparent delight.

'Maeve McQuaid! Well, I'm guessing so anyway. The red hair and green eyes from the Irish, I expect, and the alabaster skin. I got the reddy-blond hair instead of your deep red and not your lovely green eyes but my myopic and watery blue ones. Welcome!' he said loudly and grandly and came forward to envelop her in a hug.

Maeve was caught off balance and just patted him, ineffectually, on his back in return. For all he knew, she might have been a walker who had lost her way as she hadn't confirmed her identity. When he released her though, she couldn't help but smile back at his cheerful expression. Was this the mysterious person who had been left to tell her countless stories?

'Yes, I'm Maeve. Pleased to meet you – and you must be -?

'Oh sorry, Ruan, yes. Please come in.'

Come in? As though it was a normal thing to invite someone into a rundown tower, she thought. Yet, as she entered, she realised it was a house of sorts and although in obvious need of repair, it was vaguely habitable. There was an old carpet, probably an expensive one many years ago, on a stone floor. There was a table under a small window at the far side and a single uncomfortable-looking bed to her right. A fire in an old iron stove was burning to her left and a kettle simmered on the hotplate on top. A stone hearth curved around the wall and had a vent at the back of it for the outside wall. A winged chair was placed to one side of this. There were candles set on small tables next to the chair and the bed – and a large one enclosed inside a glass lantern on the far table. Maeve frowned. He didn't live here, surely?

'I do live here. Well, live and sleep here but I use the facilities at the farm such as the kitchen and bathroom.'

He had answered Maeve's question without her voicing it. Spooky or what? Was he a wizard living in his tower like Saruman - or more likely, in these conditions, was he a monk living in religious isolation? She knew though, that what she thought privately was usually written plainly on her face, however much she tried to hide it. She was the complete opposite of Beth who was inscrutable.

'Please sit down' he said, indicating the winged chair. She realised he had quite a strong Irish accent and understood the reference to their red hair now.

He carried a solid, heavy chair over from the table, struggling a little as he did. He was only slightly built and no muscles were in evidence under the loose linen tunic he had on over baggy cotton trousers. He placed the chair opposite and leaned towards her.

'Now,' he said expectantly with that same beaming smile. Nothing else was forthcoming from him and she wondered if he was waiting for her life story. She cast around for something to say.

'Your name, is it Rowan or Ruan? There seems to be a slight difference depending on who says it. Not quite like the Rowan tree.'

'Ah, the Rowan tree, the Mountain ash. Rowans are very important for warding off evil' He beamed again, then scuttled off to the table, bringing back a piece of paper and a pen.

She was beginning to think she'd been dropped into a Yorkshire version of Alice in Wonderland and wondered if Rowan was the White Rabbit or the Mad Hatter. He slid a pair of gold-rimmed spectacles down from where they were entangled in his hair.

'It is pronounced more like Ruan,' he said now. 'At least it is in Ireland. The'dh' has a ...' and here he produced a little noise from the back of his throat, 'sound to it. This is how it is spelt.'

He had been writing and held out the paper to her. RUADHAN, it said.

'So, when you say it, keep that spelling in mind and you'll get it right – as long as you ignore the 'd'.

She would have pronounced it phonetically-Ru-ad-han- and made a fool of herself if she hadn't heard it first.

'Now,' he started again, 'what do you think of our community?'

She was on firmer ground with this.

'I think the whole place is wonderful. The house, the grounds and …Beth.' She was going to say 'the people' but couldn't, in all honesty, include Glenys or Tim.

'You'll get used to the others in time,' he said as Maeve drew in her breath. Perhaps he really *could* read her mind.

'Glenys and Tim are both tortured souls but are improving every day and both have a lot of good in them. I can feel it.'

Of this, Maeve had no doubt.

'Michael, well, he can seem moody and stand-off-ish and quite scary sometimes. Mostly, it's the supreme confidence he exudes that made me feel insecure. I was nervous in his company at first but once you get over the alpha male posturing, which is all a front, he will be a good friend - as he is to me now. You just have to wait for him to let his guard down.'

'I'm not scared of him,' Maeve said, genuinely puzzled. He didn't seem standoff-ish either.

'Really?' said Ruadhan in surprise, then the smile took over his face again. 'I was a little afraid of him but maybe he's met his match with you.'

'He's just been showing me the grounds and he and Rusty have just gone for a swim in the pool.'

'In February?' laughed Ruadhan. 'He doesn't start swimming in the sacred pool until April at the very earliest. April to October usually. He's made of tough stuff but he's not a masochist. He likes a little joke. He has a strange sense of humour sometimes. He'll have been having you on.'

'But he took…'

She paused and decided not to mention the impromptu strip show. Then she remembered his laugh following her through the clearing. Her mouth set, her eyes narrowed and a flush which had more to do with annoyance than embarrassment, came to her cheeks. The words 'sacred pool' entered her mind and she jumped on them.

'You said 'sacred pool.' Why is it sacred?'

'These pools, usually next to groves, were sacred to the Druids. Well, one particular Druid in

74

this case but I can't tell you any more about that just yet. I promised Beth I'd tell you the story after dinner tonight as I forgot to turn up last night to welcome you. Many apologies.

'I got caught up in my translation,' he said, indicating the mound of papers on the table. 'I was at a sticking point. Old English can be notoriously tricky to translate. Many of the words have alternative endings and the word order isn't consistent.'

'Everyone keeps saying "Ruadhan will tell you about it" when I ask questions.'

'It's because that's what I do. I'm a storyteller and a minstrel. Did Beth tell you I'm a Druid?'

Maeve was getting used to surprises. Life certainly wasn't boring here. Ruadhan being a Druid explained a few things and brought more things up for question. She wondered if they were a secret society, like the Masons or the Society of Buffaloes. Her great-grandad had been a Buffalo. Not a sentence one hears very much…

'No, she didn't. The place is called Druid's Oak so is that anything to do with you?'

'It was many, many centuries before me, but that's a story for tonight. I'm not surprised Beth didn't tell you. She keeps her own counsel and lets people find things out in their own time. She's a wise woman and very spiritual. I think she has the gift but if she has, she keeps it to herself. We got on immediately.'

'I had that feeling too, the day I met her,' smiled Maeve.

'And I think Beth felt the same about you or you wouldn't be here.'

'So, a Druid?'

'Technically, I'm a Bard, one of the three orders of Druids. A storyteller, a poet and a keeper of traditions and heritage. The other orders were Druids as philosophers, priests, judges and educators. Ovates were the third order and they were healers, seers and diviners.'

'But they were all Druids?'

'All Druids, yes. I can't tell you any more though as I'm supposed to be telling you all this tonight.' He looked as guilty as a naughty schoolboy caught cheating.

'What about the burial mound? Can you tell me about that?'

'Ah, you've seen that have you? I *can* tell you about that but perhaps it's better if I take you up there. To see if you feel anything.'

This prompted a memory of earlier for Maeve.

'Feel as in an atmosphere you mean? Like I had at the silver birch clearing earlier?'

Ruadhan was immediately alert.

'What did you feel?' he asked, moving to the edge of his chair.

'Just a peaceful feeling. Calm. It seemed to be like a sanctuary away from the worries of the world.'

'Oh, wonderful!' Ruadhan exclaimed, jumping up. 'We think it is an ancient Druid Grove, where ceremonies were held around a central stone – or tree. You feel the same as I feel and experience what I do. Beth too. You are our *Anam Cara,* - friend of our souls. We have a spiritual connection, all three of us, now. You have a connection with the land too, your *spirit of place.* That's why you feel something there. I feel it also because I feel the place is important to me personally. Especially the glade but the whole area around it including the great oak. You said you felt the same, you loved Druid's Oak Farm?'

'Yes, I did but I'm not sure I feel it as deeply as you' Maeve admitted.

'Your gift is only young and perhaps you have never found the place to affect you this way until now.'

'I've never thought of myself like that, although I do have an affinity with the outdoors. Trees, flowers, birds…'

Ruadhan clapped his hands.

'We're kindred spirits Maeve. You, Beth and me. How wonderful!'

Oh, bless him, she thought, no wonder everyone seems so fond of him. She was just getting to her feet when he jumped up and hugged her again. Despite not being a touchy-feely sort of person, Maeve knew this was an almost child-like gesture, albeit from an intelligent, if a little quirky, off-beat person. She decided she definitely liked Ruadhan, she couldn't imagine anybody *disliking* him. That would feel like being nasty to a particularly enthusiastic and affectionate puppy.

CHAPTER 10

There were two entrances through the wall into the kitchen garden. The first took up a third of the wall space in the centre and was through a curved extension of the driveway. It was obviously for vehicular access, or carriage access perhaps in earlier days. Maeve could see the back of Bert the gardener's old blue pick-up truck to one side of a gravelled area. A smaller, arched doorway with a wooden door was to the right of this.

As she entered, she could see walls on the other three sides. There were immaculately laid-out vegetable beds to each side of a central path. She recognised beetroot and carrot tops peeping out of the ground. Leeks, onions and swedes too. Above the ground were Brussels sprouts and purple sprouting broccoli whilst cauliflower and different types of cabbage hugged the ground.

Further on there were wigwams, possibly for peas and beans and to the left were fruit cages. Espaliers were spread over each of the side walls for pears and apples, with some apples still visible.

She was now under a wooden walkway and cut-back plum and damson trees wound against each side.

As she neared the far end, she saw more apple trees on each side, surrounded by dug-over beds. These were possibly for cut flowers as some daffodils and iris were in evidence. Against the brick building to the right grew creamy-white winter honeysuckle and forsythia with its tiny, bright yellow flowers.

Approaching the large Victorian greenhouse against the back wall, she saw raised beds of thyme, lavender and other herbs before it, in various stages. The greenhouse had steps up to it and the proportions inside were immense. You could have fitted Maeve's old bedsit in here twice.

Bert was replanting seedlings into big pots on the potting benches that ran along the sides and the back. She saw Billy replacing a pane of glass to her left. He looked up and grinned his toothy grin. His hair was short back and sides but with a mass of curls on top, just like his sister's. She smiled and waved then made her way over to Bert.

Bert turned round and nodded a greeting. She had taken him for an old man before, glimpsing his old overalls and his tweed flat cap, but she could see he was younger close up, although possibly only a few years away from retirement. Do gardeners ever retire, she mused? His skin was weather-beaten and as he took off his hat to wipe his brow, she saw his hair was receding, leaving just a dark semi-circle on top.

'Hi Bert, I'm Maeve,' she smiled and he just nodded again, showing her his hands covered in compost.

'I thought as much. We don't get many people up here anymore. How do you like the place?'

His voice was quite cultured which surprised Maeve, until she realised she was making him into a stereotypical gardener with a strong local accent. Chiding herself mentally, she replied.

'I love it and I have to say, your garden is immaculate.'

He looked pleased.

'I enjoy looking after it. Nurturing it. I'm afraid the other garden, the one you'll be working on, isn't up to the standard of this one. You might have a bit of a job with that.'

'I don't mind, that's what I'm here for. Talking of which, before I buy any new tools, are there any spare ones here that I could use?'

'There are plenty tools in the tool shed,' he indicated the brick outbuildings. 'I've just given them an overhaul as it's a slack time at the moment. Some are around a hundred years old and still in good working order. They do for me but you might need to have a proper look first, both at the tools and the garden, to see if you need anything else.'

'I will thanks. I'm hoping to go into Helmsley as soon as I can to see if there's a garden centre there.'

'You could take a look at Helmsley Walled Garden. They've got a plant centre with some unusual varieties. It's not open yet till March 1st but it's not that long to wait. Don't go buying the regular plants though. I grow a lot from seed and you can make use of some of those. I always have plenty to spare.'

Maeve could well believe this as there were all shapes and sizes from tiny seedlings to what looked like small trees.

'As for any garden tools you might need, there's Naughton's hardware shop in Helmsley. They sell all the tools you'll need.'

'Thank you, Bert.' She turned to go. 'Oh, do I need a key for the tool shed?'

'No, the door's a bit stiff – that's Billy's next job today – but just go in and get what you want.'

Maeve thanked him again and went to the shed. After putting her shoulder against the stiff door and flying headlong into the place, she saw so many spades, forks, hoes and rakes that she was spoilt for choice. Most had wooden handles and showed their age but looked perfectly serviceable. Hung on the wall were shears, loppers, hedge trimmers and then a variety of other smaller tools.

She examined them all for a while, then made her way back to the house. I wonder what the car situation is here, she thought, and would I be able to borrow one? She didn't fancy the boneshaker of a blue pick-up truck but, if she had to, she'd give it a go.

As she came up to the exit, she noticed another small door on the wall to her left, half hidden by Euonymus or Wintercreeper as she knew it. Would that lead to the formal garden? She pushed the creaky wooden door open – another of the endless jobs lined up for Billy? She stood there surveying the formal garden, her domain and the mirror image of the kitchen garden in size. Formal possibly wasn't the right word for it, it certainly looked worse at this level than it did from her rooms. She turned around and shut the door with a sigh. Bert's old shears would never get through the mountains of box hedges and overgrown topiary in there. New shears and her own secateurs were essential for a start - and lots of determination. Strangely instead of feeling daunted, she was beginning to feel the first stirrings of excitement.

CHAPTER 11

The glass and walnut cabinets in the library were unlocked, as was everything else around here, including the outer doors of the house. There was a great element of trust in the community but Maeve guessed that few people would come to this out-of-the-way place to burgle it. There was only one road in and the same road out, which was more of a narrow lane with passing places. A burglar could definitely find handier places to loot.

There were plenty of valuable things to steal though, these books for a start, she thought, taking one of the leather-bound tomes from its place. She ran her finger along the bumpy spine of the book. They were mostly historical or high literature. She wanted a book to read in bed at night and these were no good unless she developed muscles like Arnold Schwarzenegger to hold them up.

She had seen some at the top end as she entered the room, which were more her style – and size. She started to close the glass door when a more modern, cloth-bound book caught her eye. She took it out. *The History of Druid's Oak Farm from the Bronze Age to Today.* Maeve looked inside and saw that 'today' was 1955 – the date the book was published. She noticed the name, Sir Edward Brabourne-Finch. Beth had said that was her grandfather's name, her mother's father. It was why her brother had been named Edward – Ned - too. Lifting it onto the table with care, she traced her finger down the contents and found what she was looking for. Chapter 27, 'The History of the Gardens and Grounds.'

She may find a few ideas for her project in here with a bit of luck. Searching the table for a piece of paper to mark the page, she caught sight of an open notebook, next to a copy of Yeats' poems. She was a big fan of Yeats. Someone had started to write one of his poems out in the notebook. She read the beautiful, copperplate writing to herself.

Your eyes so blue, they pierce my heart.
You shy away from me,
Yet I love you G.
We are so near, yet still so far apart
Until I make you notice me.

Oh dear, thought Maeve, that was definitely *not* Yeats. It was an amateur hand although she supposed the writer had managed to convey their feeling of hopelessness quite well. She wondered who –

The library door opened and a figure stood, frozen in surprise, in the open doorway. The next minute Maeve was aware of two things in quick succession. One – Glenys had written the poem and two – she wasn't in the least bit happy, to put it mildly.

'What are you doing reading my work?' the incandescent vision shrieked. 'How DARE you?'

Her voice reached such a pitch that Maeve wondered how the glass cabinets hadn't shattered. The worst thing was that Glenys was right, she shouldn't have been reading it and wouldn't have if she'd realised it was Glenys's own work.

'I didn't read anything,' said the honest person, lying through her teeth. Beth would be ashamed of her.

'Don't try and tell me that,' said the puce-coloured virago in front of her as she gathered up her notebook, pressing it to her chest like a long-lost child.

'I -I was looking for a piece of paper to use as a bookmark for this,' she held up the book as evidence, 'when I noticed the Yeats book. I love Yeats.'

This much was true at least. Remembering the handwritten poem, she must never let her know she had read it. It was too personal and Maeve would have been annoyed if it had happened to her.

'You really think I believe that?' spat Glenys.

'It's the truth,' protested Maeve who convinced herself she was only lying now by omission and the last statement was the truth.

Glenys turned on her heel and marched out, her sensible shoes stamping on the wooden floor.

Well, thought Maeve, if she didn't like me before, she'll absolutely hate me now. She knew she was in the wrong but, if she were trying to find absolution for her action, then Glenys could be blamed instead for leaving a personal poem on display in a public room.

Maeve crept upstairs to read Brabourne-Finch's *History* and contemplated locking her door behind her until the ball of fury had calmed down. Thoughts of Glenys appearing at her door with a horned helmet and a spear was incentive enough to flout the 'unlocked everywhere' rule and she turn the heavy iron key with relief.

*

'That girl is NOT going to fit in here!' Glenys was a long way from calming down just yet.

Beth looked up at her from her seat next to the fire and then stood to place the kettle back on the hotplate. After the initial disturbance to his peace, Rusty went back to his afternoon nap.

'Tea?' asked Beth, quietly.

'If I drank neat alcohol, I'd have something stronger. But I don't,' finished Glenys, lamely.

'Tea then,' said Beth, getting two china cups and saucers out. Glenys liked a proper cup of tea.

Beth busied herself and kept quiet. She would let Glenys talk and get it off her chest. Glenys slumped on a dining chair with the notebook still clasped to her chest.

'She read my poem. She was at the table reading it when I went into the library.' Glenys settled into her aggrieved tone that tended to sound like a high-pitched whine.

'You should let us read your poems more Glenys. I know you haven't got confidence in them but–'

'This was personal. She should NOT have read it.'

'And it was open on the library table, you say?'

Beth poured the boiling water into the teapot then, topped off with a tea cosy decorated with acorns and hedgehogs, she set it down on the table between them.

'Yes,' Glenys looked confused for the first time, 'I'd just popped out to use the bathroom and I couldn't have been more than ten minutes. Besides, nobody uses the library.'

'I do. Michael does.'

'But she was *reading* it!'

'What did Maeve have to say?'

'She denied it of course. What else could she do? She said she was looking for paper to use as a bookmark and noticed Yeats' book of poetry. Said she was a 'big fan' of his. Hmph'

Glenys relinquished her notebook, putting it on the table for the sole purpose of crossing her arms belligerently.

There was only one thing the poem must have contained that could have upset Glenys so much. Dear, oh dear, thought Beth. People's complicated and unresolved love lives.

'She could have been telling the truth,' offered Beth. 'That *had* crossed your mind?'

'She wasn't,' replied Glenys, her face set. She wasn't in the mood to reflect on her reaction.

Any further conversation was stopped by the arrival of Carole as she walked in the back door with a savoy cabbage in her arms. Glenys put her head down, grabbed the notebook and went through into the hallway.

'Ooh, is there another cup of tea left in that pot?' Carole asked.

'Yes, dear. Glenys didn't have one. Pull up a chair.'

'Actually, I thought I'd take it out to Tim in the barn to warm him up. Can I take some of those ginger biscuits he likes?'

Carole poured it into a mug from the cupboard, grabbed a half-pack of biscuits then went back out again.

There goes another one, thought Beth with a sigh.

*

Carole approached the open-fronted barn, humming quietly to herself. She could see the flames in the brazier, lit in an effort to keep the place warm. Yet Tim was still working in fingerless gloves, a thick jumper and jacket, and had a woolly hat pulled low over his ears. The sight made Carole want to look after him even more.

Tim looked up and saw Carole approaching. She'd seen him now so the best thing to do was just to keep still and carry on working. Escape was impossible. He cursed himself for feeling like this, for feeling the crippling shyness which had afflicted him ever since his harrowing childhood.

She was only being kind again and he could murder a cup of tea. His eyes flickered up briefly and he saw her chubby face was full of smiles. He liked the way she always had a smile on her face. He liked her eyes too. They were soft and gentle. She was altogether beautiful.

'I've brought you some tea and ginger biccies.'

He grunted, pulling the old wooden spokeshave up the beechwood branch, which was almost recognisable as a walking stick now.

'I'll put them on here so you can reach them.' She smiled at him again.

'Mm, thanks,' Tim said, not taking his eyes from the wood.

'Well, I'll just –' She pointed towards the house, turning slowly towards it. She glanced back.

I don't think he even notices I'm here, thought Carole sadly. I bet he thinks I'm so overweight that he doesn't even see me as a human being.

Tim looked up as Carole retreated at a far less jaunty pace, like she was sad.

'Damn,' he said under his breath, 'damn, damn!' And he kicked the wood shavings so that they danced around his feet.

CHAPTER 12

The library book was proving an invaluable source of ideas for Maeve. She pored over it at her table in front of the upstairs window. Seeing the garden through it helped to make planning a lot easier. Better to see it from above as at ground level it had looked overwhelming. This way, she could make a bird's eye view plan from the three full-page plans she had drawn out roughly.

She could feel the excitement bubbling up inside her. The same feeling she had when she worked at Sigwardby Hall. Not just the garden but the thrill when she had a new idea for an event. The other event organisers she worked with, largely rejected these ideas. They didn't want new ideas, even if the new ideas would have brought in much-needed income. They were a load of old dinosaurs and Maeve didn't have the influence there to push the ideas through. She was so annoyed to hear that after she left, one of her suggestions for a living museum had been taken up and passed off as someone else's idea.

She had gone for the gardening job there because, as much as she loved gardening and fresh air, she was disenchanted with being an event organiser who wasn't allowed to organise events. She had learnt her lesson though and, even when she had suggestions about the gardens, she didn't voice them, There was no point.

Now though – well, perhaps Beth would listen and surely that was all she needed. She looked at the clock, nearly dinnertime. She wasn't looking forward to seeing Glenys again. She'd been wondering about the poem and came to the conclusion that Glenys was the only 'G' here but that was taking narcissism a bit too far. Perhaps it was someone from her life before Druid's Oak and maybe the reason she came here in the first place. To get away from the mortification of unrequited love.

She left her drawings on the table and unlocked the door, leaving it unlocked. Just to show that she wasn't secretive like Glenys and that her life was an open book.

Ruadhan was going to do his storytelling tonight and she would finally hear what he had to say about the history of this place. She had just reached the bottom stair when Ruadhan himself stepped in. He was wearing a light blue, rough woollen cloak, which came down below his knees with a rough linen tunic and leggings under it. When he saw Maeve, his face broke out into the same wide, ingenuous grin that she had seen earlier.

'Maeve,' he said in his soft brogue. She wondered how anyone would hear his stories at the back of a crowd. 'I'm looking forward to telling you more about this magical place.'

'And I'm looking forward to hearing about it.'

Maeve went to hug him. She wasn't sure if she should hug a Druid but from his enthusiastic first greeting, she presumed it was okay.

They walked into the kitchen together and Glenys quickly walked out. Maeve looked across at Beth who was observing, silently.

'It's all my fault,' Maeve blurted out.

'I've heard about it and I'm sure it's not as clean cut as that,' Beth replied.

'She thinks I read her poem. Well, I did but not on purpose. I thought she was just copying a Yeats poem out until I realised it couldn't be Yeats. I daren't tell her I'd read it as I thought it would upset her even more.'

'I think that was probably a wise choice,' smiled Beth, looking quizzically at Maeve. 'You knew it wasn't a Yeats poem then?'

'Oh yes, it wasn't anywhere near as–' Maeve paused, was she being *too* honest? 'It wasn't his style.'

Beth laughed and came closer to her.

'Glenys has no confidence in her poems either but she feels like she has to do something creative to justify her place here. I think she uses them as an emotional outlet too.'

'So, she's not really a poet?' asked Maeve, her brow furrowing in confusion.

'Who is to say what a poet is? Who is to say what poetry is? What I can say is that Glenys was a very talented teacher of literature, who specialised in poetry. She also taught adult classes in poetry appreciation classes after school and they were very popular.'

'I suppose it doesn't necessarily follow that, when you know all about poetry, you will be good at writing poems. Just like you can appreciate great art even if you can't draw as much as a stick man.'

'Exactly, Maeve. Her knowledge of the poets should be enough for her and it's a shame she feels like she must do more. Don't feel guilty, she will come round.'

Tim interrupted the conversation by shuffling in and sitting down.

'Tim, can you open a bottle or two of wine for us please?' Beth asked.

He got up without a word and went to the cupboard, coming out with a bottle of Shiraz. Head down, he brought it back to the table, opening it as he walked.

Michael was next, going straight over to Ruadhan.

'Has your cold gone?'

'It's much better thanks,' came Ruadhan's answer,' but it's a wonder you didn't catch a cold yourself, swimming in the sacred pool in this weather.'

Ruadhan's ironic and straight-faced delivery was perfect and Michael had the good grace to look awkward as he glanced over at Maeve – but then he grinned. She scowled horribly back at him which seemed to amuse him. He laughed and shrugged with his arms spread in a silent plea for forgiveness. As if he cared, Maeve thought.

'Sit down everyone,' said Carole, opening the oven door, 'it's beef stew and dumplings and it's ready to serve.'

Everyone took a seat. Maeve nearly took the seat next to Tim until she realised Carole was staying and then she moved along one, leaving the space between them spare. Beth caught her eye and they gave each other knowing smiles.

'Michael, can you call Glenys please or she'll miss her meal? Go up for her if you have to,' Beth said, grabbing a dish from the worktop.

Michael looked puzzled but did as he was asked. Glenys came in two minutes later with a face like thunder as Carole took the seat next to Tim. After saying grace -Maeve remembered this time -they ate in silence for a few minutes. Carole really was a good cook, thought Maeve. Nothing fancy but full of flavour. She had just put another forkful into her mouth when Glenys spoke.

'Maeve,' she managed to say her name as though she'd actually said Beelzebub, 'told me that she's a big fan of W.B. Yeats, the Irish poet. I'm sure you'll be able to give us a few examples of his work, being such a huge fan.'

Maeve could hear Beth draw in her breath, opposite her. The others had no idea of the significance of the remarks but couldn't help feeling the undercurrents because of the tone of Glenys's voice. She finished her mouthful of food, taking her time, until Glenys looked away in satisfaction and then she spoke.

'My personal favourite is 'The Lake Isle of Innisfree' and the words that affect me most are.

'And I shall have some peace there, for peace comes dropping slow.''

She was rewarded with Glenys's head shooting up, so she continued.

'My parents, being Irish too, kept a large book of his poems on their bookshelves. That poem was my mother's favourite as well. He wrote 'Fergus and the Druid' too, didn't he?' she asked, looking across at Ruadhan.

'He did,' he replied, 'and I can sing you part of it tonight after dinner if you would like?'

'I'd love that. It's a good few years since I read it.'

Later, Maeve washed up and Glenys came over with a tea towel in her hands. She picked up a plate.

'So, you really do like Yeats then?' she asked, only a little sourly now as a note of contrition had crept in.

'I do – and there are many more poets I admire too.'

'Really?' Glenys said and then looked abashed as the remark showed, as Maeve had thought all along, that she didn't credit her with any aesthetic intelligence at all.

'Yes, Keats has been a favourite ever since school and–'

Glenys looked animated for the first time.

'Keats? Oh, I could recite his poems off by heart,' she said with something suspiciously near a smile.

'La Belle Dame sans Merci'?'

'Ah yes,' said Glenys and this time she did smile, her eyes in a faraway dream. 'A good example of unrequited love.'

As she said this, the light went out in Glenys's eyes.

'Perhaps,' started Maeve, wanting to deflect these thoughts, 'we could discuss poets and poems sometime. I'd love to know more about them.'

She held her breath.

'I think that might be a nice idea,' said the dragon, her fiery breath extinguished.

Meanwhile, the others had deserted them. Michael put his head around the door.

'We're in the sitting room when you're ready,' he said.

CHAPTER 13

Ruadhan's Story

Maeve followed Glenys into the sitting room, which had magically transformed itself into a fairy grotto. The warm, flickering light of countless candles filled the room, providing the only light apart from the fire now blazing in the grate.

Glenys went to take a place on the far sofa between Tim and Carole. Tim was already squashed up as far as he could go to one side but at the last minute, Carole slid up to him, leaving Glenys to sit at the other end. Maeve sat between Beth and Michael on the other sofa while Ruadhan perched on the edge of the chair at the side of the fire.

He held against his left arm, a strange musical instrument. Not a harp, far too small, perhaps a lyre? Maeve admired the organic carvings of trees and leaves at the base where it rested on

Ruadhan's knee. It had ten strings, fanning out towards the top where they were held with metal keys.

As she looked on with interest, Ruadhan plucked the strings and began to sing. She recognised the words of 'Fergus and the Druid', which was now set to music by the Druid sitting in front of her. The sound of the lyre was unearthly, like no instrument she had heard before. His voice astounded her. She found herself mesmerised by the perfectly pure notes.

> 'Take, if you must, this little bag of dreams;
> Unloose the cord, and they will wrap you
> round.'

As the last strains died away, she sat without moving, not wanting to disturb the charged silence afterwards. Ruadhan gently put the lyre down by the side of the chair.

'Now, for the newest member of our family, I will recount the story of Druid's Oak and how it ties in with my own presence here. It is mostly history, so if you want to make a run for it, do so now.'

Maeve smiled at him, she liked history and he knew it. She liked the idea of being part of this mostly unrelated family. She flicked her eyes to look at the others but no one moved and there wasn't even a murmur. Their eyes were fixed on the storyteller and the floor belonged to him. In a resonant voice many times removed from his normal speaking voice, he began.

'Over two thousand years ago, there were Druids in Ireland. The High Priest Druids were philosophers, judges and teachers. They taught kings. As for the Ovate Druids, the healers, the seers and the diviners, the kings sought out their help in all matters spiritual and for prophecies. Then there were the Bards. The order of Druids kept by kings to entertain them. To sing songs, recite poems, make them laugh with satire and recount the old stories of their tribes. They kept the history of the king's ancestry alive through oral storytelling, passing down from king to king, from bard to bard.

'Way back in the sixth century, one of the most famous Irish bards came into prominence. His name was Amergin. His acclaimed poem, 'The Song of Amergin' was the first Irish lyrical poem ever written. His non-anglicised Irish name, Amhairghin, means Birth of Song.

'There was still an oral tradition then. Although they had an early alphabet, The Ogham – pronounced O-am – the symbols were written, rune-like, on pieces of wood which were mostly used for divination or protection. The songs were just passed down from person to person, through generations, which accounts for the different versions people had heard and so, the words varied when they came to be written down. A little like a Druidic form of Chinese Whispers.

'Now, Amergin the bard had a family. They were not like later priests in certain religions who took vows of celibacy. I am directly descended from Amergin and his family and, although not always bards, even in recent centuries, music and storytelling have always been in our blood. My great, great-grandfather sang for Queen Victoria when she visited Ireland. My parents have died and I only have my brother and his family left. He has no interest in music, so I hope the children discover their love of music or I will be the last of the bards of this line.

'After Amergin, another great bard was born, the brother of my ancient grandfathers. His name was Dallhain. After the Romans left Britain and Christianity gradually took over the country, Druids began to disappear.

'The last of the Druidic types to fade into the past were the bards, who were retained by the royal families to keep the all-important ancestral stories alive and to provide entertainment. This was the origin of the minstrels.

'Ceolwulf in the early eighth century was King of Northumbria, which at that time extended to just above the River Humber, hence Northumbria - North of the Humber. Ceolwulf, as an educated man, studied for some time in Ireland and brought Dallhain back with him as his bard. He installed him in his timber-built Great Hall, in what is now North Yorkshire and had him entertain his retinue as he travelled between Bamburgh Castle and Mercia, further South, using the Hall as one of the stopping places.

'Dallhain remained there, along with a few retainers. The retainers lived in the Hall and Dallhain lived nearby in a tiny, wooden, one-roomed building near a sacred pool.

'The king made ever more frequent trips there, the pressures of kingship not being suited to an increasingly religious man. As Christianity became more important to him, he stayed many times on the holy Island of Lindisfarne. Eventually, he gave up his throne to serve God there.

'Dallhain continued to live here as did the few servants who were left and they lived a self-sufficient life from the soil. He asked that, when he died, he should be interred under the Great Oak along with his protective Ogham talisman to help ease his passage to the next life. Dallhain remained Pagan to his death.

'How do we know all this? We know because Dallhain the Bard wrote texts on the life of Ceolwulf and of his own daily life. I have translated this work from the Old English into modern English, which because of the unpredictability of the original handwritten texts, has taken me many years. This text, definitively places Ceolwulf's Great Hall here, on the site of Druid's Oak Farm.'

Ruadhan paused a moment for full effect. It made a marked impression on Maeve. As though she knew this place had secrets that were hidden from her. Although at the back of her mind, she knew it was the hypnotic way Ruadhan recounted the history and she could still feel the magic working. Ruadhan's eyes crinkled humorously as he saw her wide-eyed expression and he went on, gratified.

'From Dallhain's writings, we can place his hut near to where the tower is now, in proximity to the sacred pool, which is still there. The tower is a late Victorian folly but I feel closer to my ancestor when I am there.

'The original Great Hall was made of wood, cruck-framed as many Anglo-Saxon buildings were at that time, with stone foundations. The Elizabethan farm was built on the foundations circa 1572 with the two glazed extensions on either end, being added in 1732.

'The building was called Druid's Oak Farm. Sheep were grazed on the hills which then belonged to the farm. The name shows that even in the 1500s, this place was known for both Dallhain and the oak tree. The Great Oak. The oak has always been revered by the Druids and was important in their ceremonies - and it seems that Dallhain led such ceremonies here. Although he remained Pagan to his death, Paganism as such, didn't exist as a religion until Christianity came into being. The Christian religious authorities came along and outlawed other religions, which were immediately labelled 'Pagan'.

'Dallhain, therefore, wanted to be buried under his sacred Great Oak, which, according to his writings, was in direct line with the door of the Great Hall. That's my translation of it anyway, as the oak is no longer opposite the main door so, possibly when the Elizabethan farm was built and made larger, the entrance was moved accordingly. We can only surmise this.

'The Great Oak which stands outside is today known as Druid's Oak and has been named as such since written farm records began. It is, according to the written history of this place by Beth's revered grandfather, less than five hundred years old but probably replaced an earlier ancient oak which had died on the same site. It's likely that when the Elizabethan farm was built, the original oak, if diseased or dying, was replaced. Pagan ceremonies have traditionally been held around the tree for all the village, celebrating the solstices, Midsummer and other Pagan festivals. Especially May Day or Beltane for the children of the village. Although these traditions were Pagan in a Christian time, they died hard in country areas and until Cromwell, were mostly tolerated.

'In Cromwell's time, Helmsley court records state that the Oak was held to be an instrument of witchcraft, when the owner of the farm was seen 'dancing around the tree, along with others of her ilk, chanting loudly to summon the devil himself'.

'These Pagan connections, possibly starting here in the Bronze Age or earlier, continued because of Dallhain the Bard. This is why I feel close to my ancestors here- and why I feel I have come home.'

Ruadhan smiled as he said this and after a moment's pause, bent to pick up the lyre again. Everyone appeared to come out of a trance. They must have heard this story before, tonight was for her benefit, but it wasn't even about the story, it was about the storyteller. It seemed to Maeve that they had almost been held in suspended animation, mesmerised by his voice. The way you felt he was in the room alone with you, all others melting away.

'And now,' Ruadhan continued, 'I will finish with 'The Song of Amergin'.'

The fire crackled as a log fell. The candles flickered in harmony and were reflected in the eyes of the onlookers, still silently fixing the bard in their sights. Ruadhan's other-worldly voice sang the ancient song.

'Who spreads light in the gathering on the hills?
Who can tell the ages of the moon?
Who can tell the place where the sun rests?'.

CHAPTER 14

'That was an interesting night,' said Maeve to her silent travelling companion.

Michael, negotiating the narrow lanes and sharp bends in Bert's bone-shaking pick-up, threw her a quick look.

'Was that sarcasm?' he asked, defensively.

'No!' Maeve was surprised at his question. 'I love history, I love poetry, I love music. Why on earth would you think I was being sarcastic?' she replied.

'Sorry.' His face relaxed, 'I'm quite protective of Ruadhan. We all are. He appears to be – and is – a gentle, unworldly, innocent soul, yet he is massively intelligent. He comes across as an absent-minded professor archetype. If he didn't wear his own version of Druid clothing, you could imagine him shuffling around in an old tweed suit, trying to smoke a pipe that has long since gone out and searching fruitlessly for his gold-rimmed glasses, which are sitting on top of his head.'

Maeve laughed, remembering the tangled glasses. He *did* give the impression of not being in step with the modern world. 'It must be one hell of a task to translate from Dallhain's Old English,' she offered.

'Especially as Old English varies so much even when written by the same person.' He glanced across at Maeve before pulling in to let a small white van pass. Sam saluted him and got a thumbs-up in return. He pulled off again.

'He took a postgraduate course in Old English language and texts. He has a history degree from Durham and he took, not long before he moved here, an Ancient History A-level in York which appealed to him. That's where he met Kit Courtney, the archaeologist who excavated our Bronze Age burial mound. It was coming here to help later at Kit's invitation, that decided him on living at Druid's Oak. He wanted to feel connected with his ancestor. It's a bit of an obsession with him, I'm afraid.'

'I can understand the connection of place though, even though I have no ancestors from these parts. I felt it from the moment I got here and possibly even before, if that doesn't sound crazy?'

'About as crazy as Beth telling us she had written to invite you here as she knew you'd fit in. You're like the Wyrd sisters,' Michael laughed. 'You've fallen under the spell of the place. We all feel it, even me.'

'Then why don't you want it to come to you someday?' she said, more sharply than she meant to.

'For the reasons I already told you. Look, nothing is set in stone but nothing that you, Beth or anyone else says, is going to change my mind. If I stay, it will be because something has changed either within me – or with the situation.'

Maeve could see his face cloud over and realised this was a conversation he had suffered many times before. She changed the subject.

'Helmsley Walled Garden, it's closed for now I hear?'

Until the beginning of March but I can show you where it is for future reference if you like?'

'Please,' she said, hoping her smile would soften his mood. He smiled back as he pulled into the market square.

He led her through the square, up a side street and there, looming suddenly in front of them, was the imposingly tall gatehouse to Helmsley Castle.

'I remember thinking that this was the castle itself when I was a child,' she thought aloud, recalling her visit.

'Most people do,' he said, pointing to his right. 'Just follow that footpath round behind the castle when you want to visit the Walled Garden.'

After that, they both went their own way, Michael to get the paint which had been on order at the decorator's shop and Maeve to find the hardware shop. On her way, she saw a second-hand bookshop and not being the sort of person to knowingly walk past one, she went in and found three books in quick succession; a garden book, a local history book and a cosy crime mystery to read in bed.

As she was browsing the shears and secateurs in the hardware shop, she saw Michael walking towards her. He gave her a lazy smile with narrowed eyes and her stomach did a triple somersault. She took a deep breath and picked out the shears, handing them to a bemused Michael, then picked some secateurs and marched up to the counter.

'Are you local then?' the man asked Maeve after a minute while looking questioningly at Michael. Gossip was one of the shopkeeper's specialities. Michael, in turn, raised his eyes heavenward. The man's mouth twitched as he wrapped lots of brown paper around the shears.

'I'm local to Yorkshire and I suppose I'm local to the town now,' answered Maeve, 'I've moved into Druid's Oak Farm to help with the gardens.

'I could tell you had a Yorkshire accent,' he said, wrapping copious amounts of tape around the brown paper.

Maeve turned round and gave Michael her best disdainful, 'I told you so' look.

'But it was that bit of an Irish accent that threw me.'

Maeve put her head down to fish in her purse for her bank card and tried to ignore the snigger from behind her. She turned around again, to see a completely false, innocent look pop up on his face.

'Michael,' said the man, 'Before you go…'

He turned and pulled a postcard from the shelf behind him.

'My pledge,' he said, handing it to Michael, who glanced at it quickly, thanked him and went out carrying the shears.

He talked about Helmsley on the way back but made no mention of the mysterious 'pledge' and Maeve was hanged if she was going to ask him. He did, however, ask her not to mention the paint to Beth. He said he was leaving it covered over in the truck as Bert was storing it at his house for now. She was desperate to ask why it was a secret but again, she would rather suffer in silence than ask, so she just promised to keep quiet.

As they passed through Hawbury, he surprised her by asking if she wanted a drink, pulling into the car park of The Falcon before she could reply. The sun was still shining, even though it was cold and she quite liked the idea of taking in that fabulous view.

'Shall we sit outside?' she asked hopefully, aware that in February, it was usually only smokers who did this. Or dog owners but she had already seen the 'Dog-friendly' sign.

'Usually do. What would you like?'

'Half a cider please.'

A few minutes later, he came out with a bottle of the local beer 'Yorkshire Legend' and a half of cider. Putting them on the table, he glanced up and smiled at the expression on Maeve's face.

'What?' she said.

'You just look so…content, I suppose.'

She looked at the panorama in front of her. Steep grassy fields leading down to a stream in full flow after the rains. Beyond that was pastureland with woods at varying intervals and in the distance, a patchwork of fields, mostly ploughed soil at the moment. To her right, she could see the beginning of the moors which, she recalled, continued round behind Winterside Howe and up to Winterside Hill.

She sighed and sat back, picking up her glass.

'Content? Yes, I think I am. I certainly feel happier than I have in a long time. I feel like I have an aim in life whereas before, I felt a bit lost.'

'What is your aim?'

'Besides the garden you mean?'

He nodded.

'Well, I'm excited enough about that, that's my project and I'm full of ideas but…I have some more ideas too,' she said cryptically.

'Why is Beth always right?' said Michael, equally cryptically.

They considered each other silently, each mirroring the other's knitted brows and secretive expression before picking up their glasses at the same time and drinking in unison. They exchanged friendly grins at this. After another couple of minutes of taking in the views, Maeve frowned.

'Did Beth pay for the paint? I assume it's for the outside of the house? It must have cost a lot and then she has to pay someone to do the work.'

'Nosey, aren't you? Yes and no. She did pay but… sorry, there's so much to tell you and I thought Ruadhan would have told you about the mound?'

'I prefer 'interested' or 'concerned' to 'nosey' but no, he didn't get round to it but I intend to ask him. What has the mound got to do with the paint though?'

'Not giving too much away but when the mound was excavated by Kit, grave goods were found. Not rich grave goods unfortunately but still of local importance. After waiting well over a year for red tape and for the goods to be examined and go on show at the Malton Museum, Beth handed the goods over to them permanently. She received a donation from them which paid for the paint. It came at the right time as Beth's money has dwindled away to almost nothing over time. We all try and contribute as much as we can but she still insists on treating us all like a family, rather than the tenants we actually are.'

'You're family.'

'I am. You're not going to go on about inheritance again, are you?'

'Nope. What about the work though, the money for tradesmen to paint the house?'

'Not enough left over for that but we have that in hand. It will have to wait for better weather anyway but I thought we'd better get the paint now before the money for it frittered away or Beth spent it on shoring up everyone else's finances.'

There was a short pause and when Maeve turned to ask him another question, she found him appraising her. By the tender look in his eyes and the smile playing on his sensual lips, she had passed the test.

'You, I mean Beth said, I think, th-that your pictures brought in a lot of the income,' she stammered, trying to fend off the blush which wasn't a good look with red hair. 'Your paintings must be worth a lot.'

He laughed, unnerving her slightly.

'My 'pictures' that bring in the income are the photographs I take. I sell them to agencies and magazines. They're mostly of nature and the vast majority are of trees. I'm obsessed with trees in the same way that Ruadhan is obsessed with his druidic ancestry. I feel at one with them when I'm near them and I spend most of my time in the woods here or hereabouts. Even when I'm in France, I photograph trees. My paintings are mostly of trees as well but they are more personal. A hobby of sorts I suppose although I have sold a few, for much more money than I thought they were worth but I'm not complaining. That money goes towards my trips to France and the rest goes to Beth. For my keep.'

Another silence descended as Maeve thought of Michael and trees. She loved trees too – as did Ruadhan. They were a commune of tree-huggers. She had thought of Michael as a practical person and was surprised at this spiritual side to him.

She had a sudden, unwanted flash of him dressed as a Druid, sackcloth robe slashed almost to the waist, showing off the six-pack muscles of his chest. She reined back her thoughts, recognising that this wasn't the normal representation of a Druid. Could Druids even be sexy? She cleared her throat.

'A love of trees?' she said lightly, 'You should be a Druid.'

He drained his glass slowly and winked at her.

'Who says I'm not?'

Visions sprung to her mind again of the druidic muscular chest, and Michael holding forth in that wonderful deep, seductive voice of his. She quickly stood up and made for the car park with Michael following on, a bemused smile on his face.

CHAPTER 15

Beth poured her and Maeve another cup of tea from the pot.

'Are you sure you won't have one?' she asked Michael. They were the only three left in the kitchen after breakfast.

'I'm sure. I'm quite pleased with the way this painting is going and I want to get back to it before the muse deserts me.'

'That's good to hear,' said Beth and she exchanged glances with him. She knew the muse hadn't been kind to him recently.

Standing up, Michael revealed a tight black tee shirt stretched across his chest and a pair of close-fitting black jeans, skimming his slim hips. He smiled at Maeve as he closed the door and she smiled back. She glimpsed Beth raising an eyebrow and blushed, so she resorted to diversionary tactics.

'Michael's very Italian-looking, isn't he? Dark brown, almost black hair, black eyebrows and lashes and olive skin. Does he have his father's colouring?' she asked and realised that, in a bid to cover up her blush, she was now being far too inquisitive.

'No, his father Laurence, my brother Ned's son, had the same colouring as me. Anglo-Saxon blood from way back – blue eyes, fair hair, pale skin. My face has caught too much sun over the years and is now tanned and lined – but it was almost the same colour as yours when I was young.

'Michael's colouring comes from his mother. She has typically French colouring and is slim and chic, as you would expect. She has a fiery temperament too. Larry brought her and Michael up from London to live here for a while.

'Juliette didn't like it here out in the sticks and yearned for somewhere with more life. She persuaded Larry to move over to Paris, where she was born and had lived before her marriage. Michael was only five years old then and was brought up in Paris where he learnt to speak fluent French.

'I think Michael has always loved the countryside though - hence his love of trees. He often says he has fond memories of his early childhood here and always spent school holidays here with his grandfather. After he went to Edinburgh to get his degree and then his Masters in Fine Art, he reversed the order of his early years by living here and going to Paris for holidays.'

'Do his parents still live over there?'

'Juliette does. Unfortunately, Larry died just after Michael got his degree. He stayed with his mother for two months to help her get over it but age hasn't diluted her temper. Michael, being a quiet boy like his father, couldn't stand anymore and came back to live here. He visits a couple of times a year now but she has remarried, so he doesn't bear the burden of guilt over not going more. She knows she is welcome to come here to visit him but she never has.'

'So that's why he was in France when you first mentioned him.?'

'I should have explained he was back here when you first arrived.' Beth looked sheepish.

'So then I wouldn't have pulled him to pieces while he was across the table from me, you mean?' Maeve grinned.

'I think he quite enjoyed it. He appears to have this ultra-confident, even arrogant, persona – as though he won't suffer fools gladly. He's not *quite* as bad as he seems but people do tend to pussy-foot around him. You didn't – and that genuinely amused him.

*

There was no sign of Ruadhan. He had told her to come and see him in her lunch break and he would take her to Winterside Howe. She opened the tower door and called out to him with no response.

She carried on along the path to the clearing and the sacred pool, calling his name again. When silence greeted her, she stood for a moment, closing her eyes and enjoying the sweet calm that this place gave out. She opened them to look up to the sky through the feathery branches. Buds were already starting to form in this sheltered sanctuary.

Regretfully, she tore herself away and continued up to the mound. She climbed towards it, taking in the brown bracken of the moorland behind and the hill ranging behind it on the horizon. Winterside Hill, which had given its name to the Howe. She called Ruadhan's name again. Closing her eyes again, she tried to feel the history of the place, to connect with the person for whom this mound was a last resting place.

She had just opened her eyes again and was wondering if it would be disrespectful to stand on top of the mound when she heard a cough. Not a 'clearing of the throat to announce my presence' but a few wheezy coughs, like the owner smoked forty cigarettes a day.

'Ruadhan! I've been looking for you. Are you alright?'

'Just a bit of a cough. I was collecting herbs - I make tea from them - but I rushed here when I thought I heard your voice.'

He was out of breath. The short climb had obviously taken it out of him.

'There was no rush Ruadhan, I've just been soaking in the atmosphere.'

'You feel it, do you? The call of the past. Over three thousand years between then and now.'

'I can. I can feel the history around us but I can also feel that, up here, nothing has changed in all that time.'

'It's amazing, isn't it? The man who was buried here, I say 'man' because of the grave goods, must have been of some importance to have his own burial mound. The grave goods weren't of any great value but he must have been an honoured individual or leader. There were shale beads, a bone scoop, a spearhead and arrowheads and the head of an axe, made from a bronze alloy, made to fit inside a split, wooden handle. The most important find though was a bronze dagger. And of course, the pottery urn with his remains.'

'Urn? But the bones–'

'No bones. Many of the bodies were cremated until after the seventh and eighth centuries. Inhumation, the burial of the intact body, came in gradually as Christianity spread. The Christian religion thought that burning the body was sacrilegious and revealed a belief that the body would not be resurrected.'

'I had no idea' Maeve said, following Ruadhan as he turned to go down the hill again. As they came to the clearing, Maeve looked at Ruadhan.

'I *did* feel the history up there at the burial mound. I *did* feel a connection between those Bronze Age people and ourselves. Yet here,' she indicated the lush green grass, the trees and the pool beyond, 'here, I feel something else. Something more. I can't explain it...'

Ruadhan took her hands in his and smiled.

'You feel as I do. I have always felt an inner peace here. It is a sacred place. Blessings Maeve, we share a mystical understanding. A spiritual sense of place. Many people feel this but don't recognise it and it is good that you have.'

Maeve squeezed his hands and impulsively gave him a hug.

'And now,' she said, eyeing the callouses on her hands, 'back to work.'

CHAPTER 16

Maeve's shoulder muscles were stiff this morning. Her arms were aching so much that she could hardly lift them to pull her hair into a ponytail.

This brought two things to Maeve's mind. One, she was out of condition and had become unused to hard work and two, that the saying 'what brings it on takes it off' had better prove true in this case as she had an awful lot more box hedges to trim into shape with her new shears. She had the bit between her teeth now and was looking forward to getting in the garden again.

She had risen while dawn was breaking to make an early start to the day and had watched the sun come up behind the trees at the back of her walled garden.

She moved her neck a little, it hadn't seized up completely. As she glanced at the clock, she remembered Beth saying she practised yoga early in her meditation room, if anyone ever wanted to join in. She couldn't spare too much time; would a few minutes of yoga help to loosen her up a bit? There was only one way to find out.

Kicking off her shoes outside Beth's peaceful retreat, she put her head around the door. She saw the lady in question, front first on the carpet with her hands pressing against the floor and her chest and shoulders off the floor. Her head was facing the ceiling. Maeve's muscles ached just looking at her but it could be just what she needed.

'Can I join you?' she whispered.

'Of course. This is the Cobra. Try this first and then just follow me for as long as you feel comfortable.'

Beth's voice, always gentle, took on an extra layer of calm, which Maeve imagined would put any students at ease. She halted for a moment, lost in thought. Beth eyed her sideways.

'Are you alright?'

'Fine,' replied Maeve and joined Beth for fifteen minutes, by which time, she felt ready to face more Agony by Shears.

*

Sam's white van crunched across the gravel and entered the kitchen garden. Maeve had already entered through her Secret Garden interconnecting door from the formal garden. She waved to them as she watched Billy get out and collect two planks of wood from the back, walking with them under his arm towards the main house.

'Is Gil about?' asked Sam, shielding his eyes against the bright morning sun.

On receiving no answer, he noticed Maeve's puzzled expression.

'Sorry, I mean Bert. I was at school with him yonks ago and he was always Gil then.'

Maeve's puzzled expression didn't change.

'Short for Gilbert,' Sam offered.

'Oh! I just presumed Bert was short for Albert – or even Herbert. Gilbert is quite a medieval, French-sounding name, isn't it? I hope he's up there in the greenhouse as I'm collecting some Alium and Bearded Iris bulbs from him. Shall I tell him you're here?'

'No, just tell him the wife says not to forget supper's early tonight, on account of the W.I. meeting.'

Maeve delivered this message as instructed.

'Sam's given me a message from your wife.'

He looked at her sharply.

'What was it about?'

128

Maeve told him and he smiled.

'Not *my* wife, Sam's wife. She invites me round to theirs once a week. My wife died over ten years ago now.'

Oh god, thought Maeve, I'm jumping in with both feet again.

'I'm really sorry–' she began.

'Not your fault love, you weren't to know.' His blue eyes crinkled against his dark, weather-beaten skin.

'What are those?' she asked, in an attempt to change the subject. Bert's head turned towards the back of the greenhouse where she was pointing.

'The oak saplings you mean? They are very special and grown on Lady Ingram's orders. They're grown from acorns that dropped from the Druid's Oak. Those few were planted last year but those others are three years old. They're ready for a bigger pot now and they really could be planted out as we've got the newer ones but they're an insurance policy. Lady Ingram doesn't want anything to happen to the oak through disease as it is important to so many people. She wanted a replacement from the same oak, as she believed that this same Great Oak was replaced in the same way. Who knows? But there we are.'

There was a little cough from the doorway and Glenys stood there with a small tray in her hands.

'A cup of tea for you, Gilbert.'

Trust Glenys to use his full name, thought Maeve, she liked to observe the formalities.

'Lovely strong cup of tea, the way to a man's heart,' he sighed, picking up the mug from the tray.

The effect this pronouncement had on Glenys was extraordinary. Maeve looked on in astonishment as Glenys gave a wide and genuine beam of a smile, produced a high-pitched giggle and hurried out.

As Maeve carried the box of bulbs through the secret door, it suddenly hit her. Gilbert equals 'G'. Blue eyes equals Gilbert. Could Bert be the G in Glenys's poem? She grinned stupidly to herself at the elevation of Glenys to the rank of human being.

*

Taking a break from taming wild, green clumps into neat topiary orbs, Maeve wandered past the far side of the house, to where Tim worked in his barn. She knew that he would probably hate her interrupting him and definitely wouldn't want to talk to her but she was curious about what he did there and wanted to see inside the barn.

Tim looked up as she entered through the open, double doors. Strangely, although he didn't look happy to see her, he didn't seem as shy as he did at mealtimes. He returned her greeting with a grunt but his cheeks stayed their normal colour. Perhaps it was Carole's presence that made his cheeks red enough to clash horribly with his blond hair. She noticed he was wearing horn-rimmed spectacles, probably for close work. It was the first she had seen of them.

'Do you mind if I have a look around at your work Tim?' she asked. 'I'm having a rest from the box hedging. I feel like the shears are an extension of my arms at the moment and it's nice to detach them occasionally. The shears, I mean, not my arms.'

'Go ahead,' he replied, still getting on with his work. He was very sparing with conversation.

Maeve wandered around the barn. There was a collection of willow baskets, piled upon a wooden trestle table towards the back. They were all shapes and sizes.

At the end of the table were spoons - large, intricately carved wooden spoons. Were they called Loving Spoons? Next to them were a number of smaller objects which looked like they had been whittled, which included animals and birds, sitting and standing.

Above the table, dangling on strings, were wooden hearts, which always made her think of the Elvis Presley song. Then she thought how much Carole would love one of these, carved personally for her by Tim's fair hand.

She turned back towards the door and nearly bumped into a large, round metal container. The sticks inside it rattled as she steadied it. She peered closer and saw that some of the handles were plain, some had knobbly tops like the knots in branches and others represented animals and birds. These were exquisite. The heads of snakes, ducks, swans, dogs and dragons stared balefully out at her. She took one over to the doorway so she could see it better. The handle was curved over, forming the neck of a horse with its nostrils flaring, its ears pinned back and its eyes full of determination as though waiting to fly over a fence.

She heard soft footsteps behind her and was surprised to find Tim at her shoulder.

'You picked my favourite,' he said in a quietly pleased manner.

'It's so beautiful Tim, they all are. Do you sell them?' she asked, thinking how much her dad would like one of these.

'I take some to a shop in Helmsley. They take quite a bit of commission but it lets me give Beth a bit of rent.'

Maeve stared at the carved stick, though her mind at that moment was elsewhere. Tim spoke again.

'The staffs with organic handles are shillelaghs, made from blackthorn branches. They were formerly used as fighting sticks. That description always reminds me of Robin Hood and Little John fighting on the river crossing, although those would have been staffs around six feet long.'

Maeve was amazed, less at what he said than the fact that he said anything at all. She wanted to keep him talking.

'All your other work is amazing too. The whittling, the baskets, the spoons–'

'Loving spoons, an old tradition. Whittling too, that goes back to prehistoric times. Woven baskets were used by the Romans to store things or the larger ones were used to carry crops from the field. The earliest known basket was unearthed in Egypt and was found to be over ten thousand years old. Wood – used by man since they came into being, not only for practical purposes but to make toys for children and gifts for elders.

'This is why I do this. I like to think I'm following on with a tradition that was unbroken from all that time ago. With the sudden rise of technology and throwaway materials, I want to keep this going. I want to stop it from disappearing altogether.'

Tim came to a definitive full stop. Maeve stood open-mouthed but couldn't have looked more shocked than Tim himself. He looked thoroughly shaken from delivering what was probably the longest speech he had ever made. He started to back away but, before she lost him, she put her hand on his shoulder.

'Your passion shines through Tim, both in your work and in your words. You *are* keeping the old traditions alive and it's just wonderful.'

Maeve meant every word and Tim knew it. He nodded to her briefly, a ghost of a smile on his face, before going back to his work.

Wow, thought Maeve on her way back, that was a heartfelt speech. By the time she reached the garden, ideas were forming thick and fast.

*

After dinner, instead of relaxing in front of the fire with Beth, Maeve dashed off into the library and came back with a handful of A4 printer paper.

'Is it okay if I take this?'

'Of course,' Beth replied.

'What are you up to?' smiled Michael through narrowed eyes.

'Who says I'm up to anything?' Maeve replied innocently.

'Because you're bouncing about like a Kangaroo after too much caffeine.'

'I'm not,' protested Maeve.

'You are,' declared Michael.

They faced each other down for a few seconds until Maeve went pleasantly pink and a smile of triumph appeared on Michael's face.

'Well, you'll just have to wait and see then, won't you?' she said eventually, before running up to her room.

Michael stood there for a minute, still smiling at the empty space she had occupied, before turning round to Beth.

'I think I'll get back to the studio for a while,' he said before he too went out, closing the door behind him.

Beth, being an empath and the most observant of women, reflected on what she had just witnessed, then she went over to the fire and sat in her chair. Rusty jumped up from his bed to put his head on her knees, his eyes searching hers. 'I don't know Rusty,' she whispered, 'there's another pair who want their heads knocking

together – but I expect Nature will take its own
course, as usual.

CHAPTER 17

<u>The Reckoning</u>

Dinner that evening seemed to take forever. Maeve was like a cat on hot bricks and both Beth and Michael kept giving her sidelong glances.

When the last drop of rich meaty gravy from the beefsteak pie had been wiped from their plates, there was still the dessert to sit through. Homemade lemon meringue pie. Everything Carole served up was homemade from the meals themselves to the cakes, scones and biscuits for tea times and breaks. Even the bread for sandwiches was home-baked.

A big pot of coffee was standing on the table but Michael was already pushing his chair back, keen to get back to his painting. Maeve stood up before he did.

'Please, could I ask you all to stay where you are for a while longer? I won't keep you any longer than is necessary.'

Their faces all turned to her as one without a word being spoken.

'I'm just getting something from upstairs,' she said, worrying that they would all have disappeared by the time she got back. She speculated on the hushed conversation which would follow her exit. In no time at all, she was back with a folder under her arm. She opened it and remained standing while they all looked at her expectantly.

'I hope you don't mind me taking over, Beth?'

'Please do,' she smiled back.

Maeve took a deep breath.

'I have here, some ideas that I have been thinking about for the last few days. It's only a rough draft but I'd like you to give me a fair hearing.'

A few glances were exchanged and she could see they were thinking negatively already. Maeve's voice became steadier and louder now, as her determination increased.

'I'm sure Beth won't mind me saying, as I don't think it's a secret but, this house needs a lot doing to it before things get much worse. Sam was

138

in here the other day telling Beth that the whole plumbing system needs to be renewed from the original Victorian arrangement. We all know the roof wants replacing as do many of the wooden Edwardian window frames. There are so many smaller jobs out there that Billy could be kept busy for the next fifty years.

'This is all on top of the food, cleaning products and electricity bills. Not to mention council tax rates. I say 'not to mention' but I have to, don't I? Because I know we all want to pay our fair share of any bills. I know we all do our very best already. I know we all contribute what we can, however small.

'Yet even with our help, Beth's finances are dwindling, despite the windfall from Winterside Howe. I imagine you all wish you could contribute more and help out financially in other ways so we can keep this wonderful place going?'

Maeve paused. She looked at her notes, not wanting to catch their eyes. There was silence but was that just the calm before the storm?

'I propose we utilise each individual talent we possess. I also propose we make use of this house and the grounds in doing so.

'I'll start with me and what I would like to do. I would hope to have the formal garden in good order by May and at least in better shape before then. I am trying to restore it to the Elizabethan-style formal gardens that used to be here. The lines of widely spaced Linden or Lime trees will be trimmed to shape and in between, the roses on the walls will be cut right back and hopefully grow healthily again. The topiary will be trimmed into neat spherical shapes. The parterre flowerbeds surrounded by small box hedges will be planted with flowers that were used at the time, most of what we call cottage-garden flowers, such as snapdragons, sweet williams, gillyflowers, lupins, foxgloves and many more.

'As it is the first year, it will be a fledgling project but I would like to give guided tours explaining what my vision is and show them how it is being restored to its former splendour.'

She could hear a contented little sigh from Beth.

'I thought it would be a good idea to combine it with Bert's kitchen garden on a regular open day. He has agreed as long as Beth agreed too.'

She shot a quick look at Beth who nodded, still as composed as ever. She carried on, starting with Ruadhan.

'Ruadhan's storytelling talent is legendary and his singing is phenomenal. It's a shame to keep it between us.'

Ruadhan interrupted.

'Though I do both for the village at the Pagan festivities involving the Druid's Oak?'

'That would still continue as usual Ruadhan but you did say your translation of Dallhain's script was almost at an end now. So, I was wondering if we could have separate storytelling days here, with music and we could charge for them. They could be held here in the house - or in the grounds in good weather.'

'I'm very happy to do that,' beamed Ruadhan, 'after all, that's what bards do.'

Maeve could have hugged him. She turned to Michael.

'I thought perhaps you could give painting classes in your studio or again, outdoors if the weather is nice.'

She saw Michael look down, shaking his head and tried not to let her disappointment show. She had hoped he would back her up.

She ignored him and went quickly on to the next person.

'Tim. You could show everyone your love of woodworking traditions and get them involved. You could hold basket-weaving workshops with the overall charge more than covering materials and your time and expertise. And – rather than selling your products at a shop which takes most of your profit in commission, why don't you take a stall at the weekly market in Helmsley and sell your work there?'

Tim also put his head down, although she had been expecting this. He folded his arms defiantly. He didn't have to speak; the gesture spoke volumes. This really wasn't going well.

'B-Beth,' stuttered Maeve, losing confidence by the second. 'You should take up your meditation and yoga sessions again, making them open to anyone. Your meditation room is large enough to take a good few people.'

She looked imploringly at Beth, willing her to agree.

'That sounds a lovely idea Maeve. We will have to put our heads together to formulate a plan.'

Oh, Beth, Beth! Maeve could have hugged her and pinned a medal on her chest at the same time. A few heads had shot up when Beth spoke. Maeve carried on to the next person.

'Carole, I know you don't live here but Beth said you were thinking about it, to cut out journey times when you have to come up twice a day and to save going back in the pitch black of a winter's night?

'If so, your baking skills are second to none. You could charge for refreshments at various open days – or we could charge a higher rate with the food all in? Not only that, but I also thought that you could share Tim's stall on the market, displaying your cakes and pastries. They'll be snapped up.'

Carole had smiled widely as soon as sharing a stall with Tim was mentioned. Maeve had her on board now with a bit of luck – and Tim's compliance. There was only Glenys left now. As soon as that thought entered her head and even before Maeve had a chance to speak, Glenys's chair scraped back and she started to walk away from the table. From losing confidence a few minutes before, Maeve now became a different person.

'Glenys, please sit down again. I haven't finished yet.'

'I have,' came the reply.

'I'll ask you again to please sit down, as a courtesy to us all, until I've finished speaking.'

Glenys seemed so shocked by the sudden authority in Maeve's voice that she made her way, crab-like, back to her chair. Once there, she spoke again.

'And if you think I'm going to teach people how to write poems, then you'd better think again.'

Glenys's face was sour and closed up.

'I wasn't going to say that Glenys. I thought a better idea would be to utilise your extensive knowledge of poetry, to give poetry appreciation classes. Full-day courses with refreshments – perhaps in the dining room. The format would be up to you. A day of Keats? A day of the Romantic poets? Another of contemporary poets? Your choice completely.'

Glenys joined Tim and Michael in suddenly finding the floor fascinating as her gaze dropped. Maeve went on.

'And Bert is more than happy to sell his surplus plants – the ones I don't need – at all the open days. Billy says he could build a plant stall out of spare wood, just outside the kitchen garden entrance. It might not bring much in but it's better than nothing. Now,' she said, putting her head in the lion's mouth and waiting for the crunch of bones, 'who's in?'

Don't all speak at once, thought Maeve but when an answer came, she found she preferred the silence.

'I think it's a ridiculous idea.' Glenys had found her voice. 'More importantly, you are here for five minutes and think you can start calling the shots. You've got a nerve.'

Maeve measured her breathing, trying to stay calm.

'Is this how you all feel?' she asked everyone but looked pointedly at Michael.

'Painting is very personal. It is for me, at least. I don't think I can teach anyone to paint as everyone has their own style. I wouldn't even like to try.'

This betrayal slapped Maeve in the face. She didn't know why she expected his backing – but she had. She couldn't even look at him. He started to speak again but she blocked it quickly.

'Tim?' she barked, trying to drown out Michael's voice.

'No. I-I just couldn't. It's not something I do. I'm just happy carrying on as I am.'

Something in Maeve snapped. The taut band which had kept her emotions tightly contained had broken and the red-haired, part-Irish side of her broke free.

'But that's just it, isn't it?' she spat, staring deliberately into the dissenter's eyes. 'We *can't* carry on like this, can we? We can't let Beth go bankrupt, forcing her to sell this house. We can't let the house go because Beth can no longer afford to keep all of us.

'We can't keep on like we have been doing, pretending that all will be well because it won't. Not unless we start facing reality and do something about the situation.

'Glenys thinks I've got a nerve for calling the shots but it's *because* I'm a newcomer here that I can see exactly what's happening better than you.

'This place was a thriving artistic and creative community years ago – and it could be again. You don't have to follow my ideas; they were only suggestions – but you will have to do something soon or you will all be looking for somewhere else to live. What's more, so will Beth. She will lose her family home. Do you really want that on your conscience?'

Maeve sat down with a bump, folded her arms and then glowered at all the shocked faces around her. Beth silently appeared at her side, kissing the top of her head. Then she addressed the small audience.

'When I first met Maeve, I had a good feeling about her. Yes, we got on immediately and she seemed like a nice person but also showed she was full of energy and ideas that she hadn't been able to put to good use. I hoped that by inviting her here, I could let her have the space to create these visions and give free rein to her ideas. And, hopefully, help me see a way out of this situation we find ourselves in. She has not let me down.

'All these ideas she has suggested are practical and more than that, could easily be put into practice without costing us too much money.

In fact, we could make enough money to give us hope, at least. I urge you all the objectors to think carefully about them because, above all, Maeve was right. If we don't start making more money, we may not be able to hang on to Druid's Oak Farm for much longer.'

This calm measured speech had even more of an effect on them than Maeve's tirade because it was unlike Beth to talk about these matters. Maeve knew, as did Beth, that something in the perception of those listening, had fundamentally shifted.

Michael cleared his throat.

'As I tried to say earlier before being given the cold shoulder,' he said, looking pointedly at Maeve, 'I won't teach painting – but I will hold photography days, taking them in the grounds to photograph wildlife, trees and nature in general, which this place has in abundance.'

He caught Maeve's eye as he finished and she had the good grace to look ashamed. Carole spoke up.

'I can put some of my baking on your stall Tim, displayed in some of your baskets. Maybe some of Bert's plants could go into the smaller ones too? When it comes to your woodworking open days, I can explain the processes to people as you are working on the crafts.'

Tim looked up at her through his fringe, the ghost of a smile on his face. He gave the faintest of nods and a whispered 'thank you' but it was enough for Carole to look like she had won the lottery.

Now there was only Glenys who swallowed audibly, the pride getting stuck in her gullet. Eventually, she spoke.

'I suppose there is a conversation to be had.'

Which was the Glenys equivalent of waving a white flag. Beth pulled Maeve up and hugged her warmly.

'There are many conversations to be had,' said Beth, 'and many thoughts to turn over in our heads. Let us all think it over and meet in a few days to discuss things. Well done, Maeve.'

There were murmured agreements at this and a cheer from Ruadhan. Over Maeve's head, Michael caught Beth's eye. She had known from the start that Maeve would come up with something like this, he thought. Mystic Meg had nothing on his aunt.

CHAPTER 18

Spring

Spring had arrived early at Druid's Oak Farm. As Maeve sat on the bench outside the kitchen window, she surveyed the results of her hard work - of cutting back, pruning and clipping. Rusty sat by her side after first completing his circuit of the garden in search of a good old sniff.

It was weeks now since she had arrived here and the garden was almost unrecognisable. Climbers were already in bloom over the bower at the far end and the flowers she had planted were coming up just in time for the Open Day on March 21st, which was this year's Spring Equinox.

The box topiary was trimmed into perfect spheres and the low box hedging enclosed all the flower beds, which had Tudor-style flowers growing in them.

The fountain in the centre was a silent pool of water with an octagonal stone structure in the middle of it. It reminded Maeve of a baptismal bowl in a church. On the open day, the water would fall out over the pool in a gentle spray but for now, the pump was switched off.

The small, double blooms of Rosa Alba climbed up the walls, their fragrance catching you as you walked past them. The stronger scent of wallflowers, known in Elizabethan times as Gillyflowers, would greet their guests as they entered the garden. They were planted in three large stone bowls, at the tops of the central pathway and the two smaller ones as well as in the flowerbeds.

It would be a local open day as the visitors were mostly from Hawbury village – the same people who traditionally attended the Pagan ceremonies. It seemed only right that they should see the new/old garden first. Besides, thought Maeve, it would be a good test run for the later open days, with people coming from a wider area, hopefully.

She had done all she could do for now and she was happy with it. Even Bert was impressed and Beth's eyes had looked quite watery as she praised Maeve's vision.

The Elizabethan Garden, as it had now been christened, as a nod to Beth as well as the style, was an ongoing project - and one she was looking forward to now that the tidying-up work had been done. She picked up the empty coffee cup by her side and entered the house through the kitchen door.

Carole was ruddy-faced with the heat from the oven as she had been baking non-stop. The Spring celebration was two days away and everyone was ignoring the met office's forecast from Hell. They predicted severe rainstorms over a two-day period. Rusty trotted over to her, looking up at her through imploring eyes. Carole relented and gave him a tiny bit of meat, destined for the pies.

'What will you do if it rains and all this food is wasted?' Maeve played Devil's Advocate.

'It will never be wasted, not in this house. I can just freeze it anyway and we'll eat it later. But stop thinking like that! You're the one who's encouraging us to look on the bright side, so follow your own advice.'

Maeve laughed. They all seemed fired up now, even Tim and Glenys. Tim was displaying his wood and basket wares inside the barn and Glenys was helping him out with any sales, as Carole would be busy with refreshments at first.

Glenys had embraced Maeve's suggestions, after two days of sulking and a sharp talking to by Beth. She planned a 'Romantic Poets Day' here before Easter and had also applied to help adults with their English literacy at Helmsley College. She had come into the kitchen looking as happy as Maeve had ever seen her, waving the formal reply of acceptance from the college.

If ever Maeve had doubts about bulldozing people into going along with her ideas, she thought about Glenys and how it seemed to be bringing her back to life – and she doubted no more. She had even received a smile and a thank you from Glenys and an invitation to sit in on her first Poetry Day here.

Michael and Beth had both held their test-run open days last weekend, at either end of the house. Lunch was in two sittings in the kitchen so their paths didn't cross. Luckily, it had been a sunny, if cold day and Maeve had seen eight people, cameras in hands, congregating around the Druid's Oak as well as on the edges of the woodland. It was early days yet and they had both only advertised it locally in the library and shops but these things were often helped by word of mouth as much as advertising.

Ruadhan was like her, waiting for the Spring equinox – or Alban Eilir as he called it. This was a

Druid celebration, known also to pagans as Ostara, at the midway point between Imbolc and Beltane. He refused to charge money for something that had always been a traditional gathering for the locals but would again use it as a test run for other storytelling days.

He had planned an evening celebration too with his ritual blessing of the great oak, which brought with it, good luck for the coming half-year. They would follow that with a bonfire on the piece of ground that Bert used to burn any un-compostable garden rubbish.

Maeve was just going to let the visitors wander in and out of her garden whenever they wanted. She had asked Billy to make sure the benches dotted around there were solid enough to sit on so people could just get away for some quiet contemplation if they so wished. She would be there for them to ask any questions and she had printed out information leaflets, which she would leave around the place, in the barn, at the food stall and mostly on Bert's plant selling stall.

Michael and Beth would be doing their social hosting duties but would also be relieving the others so they could enjoy the day too. Maeve was looking forward to seeing this famous tradition in practice and to hearing Ruadhan's hypnotic singing voice again. Apparently, he sang the more established early folk songs at these gatherings, such as 'Jack in the Green' and 'Follow the Plough' so that everyone could join in with them - and his stories were tailored towards the children.

After checking with Bert that things were all in order for his plant stall and kitchen garden tour, she headed off towards Ruadhan's tower, with Rusty excitedly showing her the way. Ruadhan was Rusty's favourite person. Ruadhan was everyone's favourite person.

She heard the noise before she saw anything. A tap-tapping noise, echoing around the trees. Then she saw Michael on top of the tower roof, hammering a couple of slates in place although, like with the farm, it would be like putting sticking plaster over a tiny part of a colander.

'Busy?' she grinned up at him.

'Trying to provide a bit more cover because if the biblical-style rainstorms do happen, I don't think Ruadhan will have enough buckets and bowls.'

The man in question came from around the back of the tower and dog and Druid greeted each other exuberantly, then Ruadhan looked up at Maeve.

'But it isn't going to rain because we have everything planned down to the last detail, so it wouldn't dare, would it Maeve?'

His laugh turned into a cough and Rusty licked his hand as Michael threw a worried glance towards Maeve.

'The damp in this place isn't good for you, you know,' Michael shouted down, 'and there are more slates that need replacing when we can find some that match.'

'I'll be fine now you've mended the one over my bed, thank you, Michael. Now, how does your garden grow, dear Maeve?'

'It'll do,' she replied with a grin, employing the standard phrase used when you were really happy with something but were too Yorkshire to show it.

'Come inside and we'll drink a toast to the success of Alban Eilir and our new enterprises.'

'Oh, a glass of champagne from your secret stash, Ruadhan?' asked Michael, tongue in cheek.

'Oh, sorry, it's just tea. Will that be alright?'

Michael jumped off the last rung of the ladder and put an arm around Ruadhan's shoulders.

'I was joking. Tea is good. Will you never get used to my sense of humour?'

'When you find one, we'll let you know,' said Maeve, following them in accompanied by Rusty and a filthy look from Michael.

CHAPTER 19

The day of the Spring equinox dawned deceptively brightly. Despite dire warnings from the Met office, the last couple of days had been dry. The celebrations were still set to be held in the grounds and the people of Hawbury were expected within the hour. Quite a few had turned up early to help.

Leaving the garden leaflets on Bert's plant stall, which also had a large marker pen arrow pointing to her garden, he spoke in a low voice as she passed him.

'Can you feel something in the air?' he asked her. 'The birds are acting strangely and - well, it's a bit warm. For the time of year, I mean. Not a breath of wind either.'

'I'm sure it will be okay Bert. Look, not a cloud in the sky?' she smiled.

Bert knew his weather lore though, she thought as she walked off, then she noticed that the birds, always making a noise in the trees, were suspiciously silent. She shrugged it off.

There were visitors here already, parking their cars along the wide drive coming up from the road and more were arriving as she watched. Birds could possibly sense a disruption to their routine as much as dogs did. Rusty certainly hadn't gone silent though. As soon as the first people walked through the entrance to the grounds, he made it his personal responsibility to greet everyone enthusiastically, a permanent 'smile' on his face.

As some of the visitors made for Bert's stall first, she saw him bring something up from under the table. She went a bit nearer. It was a box with 'PLEDGES' written on it, in the same marker pen as the arrow. Maeve frowned, what *were* these pledges? The man at the hardware shop had handed one over to Michael a while ago.

Beth shouted to her, stopping any investigation, asking her to take some of the plastic boxes she was carrying before they toppled. There was food in them ready to put out on the gingham cloth-covered trestle tables on the food stall. Michael was there setting up and in case the met office was right for once and it did rain today, the stall was covered by a tarpaulin on poles. Carole started transferring the food from the boxes onto large platters, covering them with clingfilm for now. There was the traditional Spring celebration special of lemon and honey cake. Asparagus flans and spinach and goat's cheese individual tarts were displayed now, along with flaky sausage rolls, meat and potato slices and creamy chicken pasties.

Everyone else had brought sandwiches, buns and crisps for their picnics. Vik, the landlord of The Falcon had brought crates of the local ale. Sam's brother from the grocery shop had brought some bottles of homemade mead, which, according to local legend, would most likely blow your head off.

It wasn't lunchtime yet however and most people were making for Bert's plant stall, with a few wandering over to Tim's barn. With a jolt, Maeve realised they were also making for her Elizabethan Garden and she raced over there to be on hand for any questions.

There were folk walking up and down the garden for nearly two hours., bending for a closer look, pointing up to the topiary and the roses and asking Maeve lots of questions which, thankfully, she could answer. She had some wonderful feedback which had her grinning from ear to ear. It seemed to be a success already and it wasn't even finished yet.

Bert's kitchen garden tours were going very well too and Billy, manning the plant stall, had almost sold out. Carole had left the food stall by now, leaving her mother in charge, so was now in full flow in the barn, praising Tim's passion for the old woodcrafts as he blushed and kept his head down whilst weaving the baskets.

Glenys arrived to take over at the garden so that Maeve could get something to eat and have a look around. Glenys said she had seen it all before and wasn't much for Pagan celebrations, having been brought up 'chapel' but was happy for other people to celebrate how they wanted and always joined in to show solidarity.

Maeve looked over at the vast lawn in front of the house and saw it was now dotted with families and couples sitting on blankets, finishing off their picnics. Some of the older Hawbury residents were seated on chairs brought from the kitchen. The chairs were placed in front of the house to give them a good view of the proceedings.

When everyone had almost finished eating, the music started up. Maeve was surprised to see Michael playing the guitar. She was even more surprised to see Beth playing a deep-noted tenor recorder and was absolutely gobsmacked to see a ruddy-cheeked and obviously uncomfortable Tim join in with a Bodhran, beating different rhythms for each song.

After a while, everyone packed up their blankets and came to listen to the traditional folk songs being played by the trio, who had obviously played together before. Maeve ran back to take over from Glenys but found her sitting peacefully on a bench with her eyes closed. There were only two elderly people in the garden now, so she told Maeve to go back and enjoy herself.

Maeve rejoined the people congregated around the trio. After a few minutes, Ruadhan came over and caught hold of Maeve's hand, dancing in the direction of the Druid's Oak tree. Someone caught hold of Maeve's other hand and, before long, there was a snaking line of people, all going three times around the oak tree and off around the grounds.

Everyone was out of breath and laughing when the music stopped. Ruadhan led them all back to the oak. There, as Michael came to hand over his lyre harp, Ruadhan the Bard began to play, his voice soaring with the angelic chords of the instrument. His beautifully pure singing voice held them all in thrall. The bard in front of them was confident of his natural gifts and no trace of the shambolic, sometimes scatter-brained person remained. Michael came round to stand next to her.

'What do you think of our heathen ways then?' He bent down and whispered in her ear, sending a pleasant shiver right through her.

'I think your heathen ways are very entertaining. I loved the Druid version of the Conga.'

He smiled at her and they turned back towards Ruadhan, listening to the end of the songs. His voice had perfect pitch; it was unique. As Ruadhan finally laid his lyre harp against the oak, Michael nudged her.

'Watch this,' he said, nodding towards the children who were breaking away and sitting on the grass directly in front of Ruadhan. The grown-ups remained behind them. Everyone obviously knew this ritual off by heart.

Ruadhan moved in front of them like a dancer as they fixed their eyes on every dip of his body, on every inclination of his head and on his arms, which were gracefully expressing the words he spoke.

After hearing the second of the three stories, which she enjoyed every bit as much as the children did, Maeve reluctantly dragged herself away from the bard and his rapt audience and headed back to the Elizabethan Garden. She had to drag herself away from Michael too but she tried not to dwell on what that meant.

As she crossed the lawn, she glanced up at the sky. The blue had disappeared, to be replaced with a misty mauve. A strange sky with a strange feeling. She was feeling now what Bert had felt earlier. Still, it was warm – unseasonably warm – and dry, so that was all that mattered today.

Glenys, she noticed as she went back into the garden, was very good at dealing with the public. It wasn't what Maeve had expected from her antisocial persona when she first arrived. Yet she had dealt with the pupils and the public on a day-to-day basis at her school so it followed that she knew how to conduct herself. She came over to Maeve and smiled broadly. Maeve had to fight the sensation of providing amusement for a crocodile before it ate her.

'Your garden is very popular. Everyone was interested in the restoration and the information in your leaflets. They said it was a calm, zen type of garden. You should be very proud of yourself.'

Maeve was astounded, not so much at the views people had expressed but that Glenys was singling her out for praise. She put her hand on Glenys's arm and squeezed.

'That means a lot Glenys. Thank you.'

Ten minutes after a smiling Glenys had left the garden, a breeze started up. Then it strengthened into a wind, whipped up from nowhere like a sandstorm in the desert. The turbulent wind continued for the next fifteen minutes and people could be seen looking up at the sky and shaking their heads. Then the first drops of rain began to fall as the sky darkened to a threatening indigo hue. Large drops splashed onto the ground, gradually getting heavier as the gardens emptied of visitors shouting their goodbyes over their shoulders.

On her way to help with the stalls and chairs, Maeve bumped into Bert.

'This is set to be a bad'un,' he said as they both ran to contain the food stall's flapping cover, which was in danger of flying off over the grounds.

Some of the villagers had taken shelter in the barn but, as it became obvious that this wasn't just a shower, the last of them left. The ones who had walked up here got lifts in cars that were packed to the brim, shouting thank yous and goodbyes as they went. Soon, the residents of Druid's Oak Farm were left alone.

'I suppose that means the bonfire is off then?' asked Ruadhan, still with a look of hope in his eyes, not unlike Rusty's when he was waiting for some crumbs of food from the table.

'It most certainly is,' said Beth. 'Just look at that sky.'

It was swirling around above the house as though a black hole was about to open up.

'I haven't done the blessing ceremony on the oak yet. The one that ensures luck for the coming season.'

'Well, you won't be doing it now Ruadhan – and we make our own luck,' said Michael.

Beth frowned at Ruadhan.

'And you must sleep here at the farm tonight. Our roof is bad enough but there is nowhere for you to escape in your tower if the rain comes in.'

Ruadhan produced the mild version of a sulky face.

'I mean it Ruadhan,' Beth said sternly.

'Is it alright if I stay here too?' asked Carole. 'I didn't go back with the others as I wanted to help clear up.'

'Of course it is, you know you are welcome to stay any time – or even permanently.'

'I meant to say,' said Michael. 'Vik from the Falcon invited us all there to continue the celebrations. First time in years that they've been cut short.'

164

Nobody fancied driving down in the deluge now falling in sheets from the sky, so they all went about their tasks; clearing, washing up, wiping down and putting what little food was left, in the fridge. Michael lit a fire in the sitting room and, an hour later when everything was done, they made their way through there.

'It was still a good day though, wasn't it?' asked Maeve. 'A success, I thought?'

'Everyone enjoyed themselves even if it was curtailed. There was only the blessing and bonfire missing,' agreed Beth.

By the time they sat down in front of the fire, the first rumbles of thunder could be heard.

CHAPTER 20

I trace, three times three, a circle in this sacred place.

*

The second growl of thunder was much louder. The storm was getting closer. They could hear the gale-force winds rattling the windows and making
their way down the chimney with a low moaning sound, like the ghost of Jacob Marley.

Rusty wouldn't settle. He was barking and whining. Beth thought he was just unsettled by the storm but then why would he be barking at the front door as if he wanted to go out in it?

*

Banish the dark and bring light into our world.

*

The next minute, the room lit up with a stark white flash of lightning. They all looked at each other without saying a word. Fierce storms like these somehow brought out a deep-seated, primaeval fear in their psyches. Beth's face suddenly changed.

'Where is Ruadhan?' she said. 'Has anyone seen him?'

'He brought all the writings and books up earlier,' Glenys answered. 'They're on the desk in the library. So he must intend to stay here. He might have gone upstairs to his room,' she finished, in an attempt to stem Beth's anxiety.

'Michael–'

'I'm on my way. Is he in the next room to Tim's?' He was already moving towards the hallway door.

'He is. Hopefully.'

Beth smiled but it didn't reach her eyes.

*

Hail, Guardian Spirits of the Tree, we ask you to bring peace and plenty to this place.

*

Another crack of thunder, followed a few moments later by a prolonged flash of lightning. Glenys went over to the window.

'Be careful,' said Maeve, only half in jest, stemming from a half-remembered superstition as a child. 'They say that if lightning strikes at the

167

window, it captures your soul and leaves your reflection imprinted on the glass.'

'Where on earth did that come from?' laughed Beth but the laugh was cut off short by Glenys's exclamation.

'Oh my god!'

'What? What is it?' Beth and Maeve went to join her whilst Carole and Tim went to the next window. Beth gave a cry of alarm.

'What on earth has possessed him?'

Michael came back to the room, ran to the window and then ran straight out again.

'Be careful,' came Maeve's small voice.

Opening the front door, Michael could see the pale robes of Ruadhan as he circled the Druid's Oak. The next crack of thunder shook the house and two seconds later, forked lightning jumped around the sky as though searching for somewhere to earth. He could hardly see anything through the rain, which soaked his shirt as there was no time to put a coat on.

Michael kept watching as he ran and thought he could see Ruadhan's lips moving as he got closer. He watched as Ruadhan's movements slowed and he leant against the great tree, his forehead touching the bark. Michael didn't recognise that as part of the ceremony. He ran full pelt towards the tree.

Sacred Spirit of…Sacred…Spirit…

Ruadhan was gradually sliding towards the ground as he tried to speak. As Michael reached him, a clap of thunder above almost split his eardrums and – at the same time – a jagged, malevolent surge of lightning finally found somewhere to earth its power.

As Michael looked above him, he saw and heard the lightning slice through a huge branch as if it was butter. He felt an electrical urge under his feet and saw that the noise had brought Ruadhan around and he turned his ghostly face towards Michael.

The awful cracking noise from above had nothing to do with lightning as Michael saw the branch tearing away from the trunk. He knew he had to get Ruadhan from under there – and quickly.

He grabbed the weak and unresponsive figure and began to half-drag, half-carry him away. He had barely made any headway when the huge limb finally parted from the tree with a groan which sounded like all the tortured souls of hell.

Almost sure that the branch would fall on them now, he pushed Ruadhan away and threw himself on top of him. A second later, he felt the

169

full force of it on his left-hand side as it hit him. He knew that the branch had only caught him a glancing blow but it was enough. In the state Ruadhan was in, it could have killed him. He tried to stand up but his ankle gave way. He fought the pain and tried again, this time trying to drag Ruadhan, who was still lying prone on the sodden grass, to a standing position. Just as he realised this was impossible, a large figure appeared and bent down to scoop the half-conscious Ruadhan up in his arms. Tim shouted against the tumult of the night.

'Can you make it back?'

Michael nodded and started to limp towards the house and its open door, crammed with anxious figures. One of them broke away, running towards him and placing themselves under his arm.

'Lean on me,' yelled Maeve.

Michael looked down at her, rain and mascara running down her face, hair flattened against her head – and thought that she had never looked more beautiful.

CHAPTER 21

The doctor had been called. No one ever expected a doctor to visit these days. One could hardly get an appointment with them during the day, let alone a home visit at night in the worst storm in ten years. This doctor though was Dr Ardley and had been the family's doctor throughout his long career, as well as being a personal friend of Beth's.

'Ruadhan should have come to see me long before things reached this stage. What possibly started out as a chest infection has now developed into pneumonia. Hopefully, this can be treated with antibiotics and I am putting him on a drip straight away. I'm not going to beat about the bush, if we've caught it in time, he should be all right, if not, it could be life-threatening.'

Everyone standing around the room felt the burden of guilt keenly, even though, realistically, they knew that they had tried their hardest to get him out of the damp tower. Ruadhan's need to be near his ancestor had brought the likelihood of his joining him, much nearer. The crazy action of carrying out a sacred tree blessing in the middle of an apocalyptic storm was something that none of them could have predicted. What was he thinking?

They watched as he tossed and turned on the white bed sheets, kicking the duvet off, oblivious to his actions. His already slight frame looked wasted and his face was white, with a livid stain of red, high on each cheek. He muttered unintelligible nonsense.

'Not finished. Not finished.'

Was he talking about the blessing ceremony?

Beth looked at him. She hadn't had children but this must be what it felt like to worry about a stubborn, contrary son whom she still loved dearly because he was the most kind, gentle and loving person she had known. She felt her heart being torn out of her. Suddenly, his eyes opened and fixed directly on hers.

'Must – must – finish. Do. Blessing. M-MUST,' he croaked, then fell back onto the pillow as his eyes closed and his arms fell to his sides.

Carole burst into tears, which set Maeve off.

'Is he…?'

The question hung in the air as the doctor bent towards him.

'No, he's asleep. A deep sleep is the best thing for him at the moment,' he replied as a collective sigh of relief escaped the gathering. 'He's not out of it yet by any means. He needs to be watched throughout the night and tomorrow too. Ring me if there is any change for the worse.

'I will get a few hour's sleep and I'll be back up here mid-morning. Until then, keep checking the drip. Keep the room warm with the heater but don't light the fire, the fumes won't be good for his chest and his breathing.'

With this, the doctor took his leave of them, pulling Michael out with him to tend to his injuries in the kitchen downstairs.

*

Beth, of course, had said she would sit with him first. Glenys said she would stay with her for support and the gesture was appreciated. They had company in their vigil, in the form of Rusty, who wouldn't leave Ruadhan's side and resisted all attempts to let him out. He was an immovable object – his eyes focused solely on Ruadhan's face. Dr Ardley had told them to let him stay and that dogs were good at helping patients get better by their devotion alone. It was almost an attempt at telepathic communication on the animal's part. Besides, he had tried his best to let these stupid humans know that Ruadhan was out in the storm in the first place.

Downstairs, Dr Ardley had diagnosed Michael's badly sprained ankle, although at least it wasn't broken. His back was badly bruised along the left-hand side. He had also managed to sprain his left wrist, although he hadn't been aware of the pain until a while after it happened. His focus had been on Ruadhan. The doctor treated the joints with a cold compress and then bandaged them for support. As he went out of the house, he turned to Michael.

'Quite a night!' he said, in what was probably the understatement of the year.

The residents of Druid's Oak Farm formed a metaphorical queue to sit with Ruadhan. When Maeve had taken her turn with him for three hours over breakfast time, the two red dots on his cheek had disappeared and he was deathly pale. His breath was drawn out of him in strangled gasps and, for the first time, Maeve began to think that he might not make it.

'Come on Ruadhan,' she kept telling him. 'You can make it. Keep fighting.'

The tears fell unchecked down her face as Rusty, as still as a statue, kept up his vigil.

CHAPTER 22

Breakfast, for Maeve, was a solitary affair, coming as it did at mid-morning. No one had an appetite and Carole had stopped trying to make people eat. She was now sitting with Tim in Ruadhan's room. When Maeve had left for them to take over, there had been no change in him. She had heard Dr Ardley arriving a few minutes ago and Beth asking him in the hallway if he wanted a hot drink before she accompanied him up the stairs.

Maeve stopped trying to force toast down her dry throat and poured herself another coffee instead. She had caught sight of herself in the hall mirror and saw her eyes were puffy and red and her hair was stuck out like a lion's mane – and she didn't give a damn. What did that matter now?

The storm had raged for almost two hours. Just when they thought it had stopped, it seemed to start up again as though it was moving around in circles. The rain, still bouncing on the ground until an hour ago, had stopped abruptly. Now, just the slow drip of rogue raindrops could be heard falling outside the windows. At least she hoped it was outside. The leaks in the thatch had let in rain in far more places than ever before. Every bowl, pan and bucket had been pressed into service. Ruadhan's tower would be a wreck.

Maeve's train of thought stopped abruptly. She ought to go there and see if anything needed saving. Glenys said he had brought the copies of Dallhain's original manuscript into the library, along with Ruadhan's own work – but what about clothes, shoes, books?

She stood up and went to put on her waterproof coat and boots. She looked around for Rusty, so she could take him with her but, of course, he was still upstairs, guarding, waiting.

The air outside had that unique quality of renewal after a storm has passed. The smell of the earth filtered up through the still-soaked grass. The sun was creating a silver lining on the clouds and the wind had dropped completely. The only movement was the journey of raindrops held inside the nearby shrubs, now dripping very slowly to the soil below.

Maeve's eyes were drawn to the great oak. Druid's Oak. The massive branch was still lying to the left side of the tree and was now dying, ripped from its sustainer. Ruadhan would be devastated, she thought – and her heart thudded. She hoped he would have the chance to be devastated. It was far better than the alternative.

She approached the oak head-on, noticing as she did that the tree didn't look as lop-sided as it should. It was the lowest, heaviest branch on that side that had been torn off and strangely, as the branch had reached out further than the rest, it looked almost symmetrical now. As she passed, she could see the raw wood inside where the bark had been torn from the tree. The branch itself was almost split in two lengthwise too as though the lightning had travelled along. Last night, from the doorway, it had looked like the whole tree was exploding.

Suddenly, she wanted to pray for Ruadhan. Pray to who or what, she didn't know as she hadn't prayed since she was a very young child. She should pray to the old gods, the gods of nature, of trees, of rock, of air and of water. That's what Ruadhan would do if the tables were turned and straight away, she knew where she should be.

Running now, she reached the grove, the clearing surrounded by silver birches where both she and Ruadhan had felt some transcendent sensation. She saw the pool, water cascading down into it, in full flow because of the storm. The noise, though much louder than usual, was somehow soothing. It showed the power of nature as much as the lightning-struck tree did. She didn't go any further than the middle of the grove, to where she had felt the power when she first came to this place.

Ruadhan had explained about the Sacred Groves where Druids held their ceremonies. They were surrounded by trees, which were usually oaks and he had said there was a central stone - or a tree. The stone was either a standing stone or a slab. Or two stones with a larger stone across them like a table, used for rituals or sacrifices in the very early days. She put that out of her mind in the certain belief that this peaceful place had never been used for blood sacrifices. It just seemed so magical here.

She saw the toadstools growing in a ring around a darker green circle of grass.

'Never enter a fairy ring'

The childhood warning still echoed in her head but right now, she knew it was the right thing to do. She felt as though someone was guiding her. She moved forwards into the ring and wasn't immediately transported to Fairyland, although it did have a powerful effect on her. She closed her eyes and absorbed her heightened perception of

Nature. Every smell, every movement, every sound.

She stayed there for a while turning in her own circle within the circle. She opened her eyes and looked up through the surrounding trees, which seemed to be leaning in towards her as if waiting to see what she would do next.

'Please. *Please,*' she said out loud.

'I appeal to all the gods that Ruadhan believes in, to help him now. Please make him better. Don't let him die. I appeal to his ancestors. To Amergin. To Dallhain. Look after your son and bring him back to us, healthy and happy.'

A flash of memory – Ruadhan's beaming smile and his intelligent yet innocent eyes, brought a lump to Maeve's throat.

As she opened her eyes, she looked down at the toadstools enclosing her and something stirred. Another memory from the years before she came here, at the estate. Toadstools. Fairy rings. A memory too of what Ruadhan had told her about Druid groves. 'A central stone – or a tree.' *Or a tree.*

*

Before she could reach the house to make a phone call, Maeve saw Dr Ardley coming out of the door, accompanied by Beth and Michael.

179

'How is he?' Maeve almost yelled; her eyes wide.

'He's a little easier now the fever has subsided. He's still in a deep sleep, which he desperately needs. I'll tell you the truth, I thought I would be sending for the ambulance this morning but there's no need to move him yet unless he deteriorates.

'The crisis is not quite over and he will need constant watching for signs of improvement. I will be back in the morning to change the drip if need be but I have high hopes he may be able to take the oral antibiotics I've prescribed by then. For now, just let him sleep and try not to worry, he's stronger than he looks.'

'We're lucky to have you as a doctor – and a friend - and I can assure you that Ruadhan is not going back to live in that damp tower. I should have put my foot down before,' said Beth.

'My dear Beth, we both know that Ruadhan goes his own way – but this might have taught him a lesson.'

Michael limped over to Maeve and drew her to one side.

'That looks painful,' she said, nodding at the ankle. 'And the wrist?'

'And the whole of my bruised and battered left side but it was worth it to know that Ruadhan is showing some small improvement.'

'I agree, though it's easy to say that when it's not me who's suffering,' replied Beth.

'I wondered if you could run me into Helmsley tomorrow to get the medication and a few other things. I don't think I could manage to drive.'

'Of course I will. I want to do something useful.' Maeve looked back at the house. 'Is Rusty...?'

'Still at Ruadhan's bedside, yes. Although he's now asleep by the side of the bed, so I think he realised that Ruadhan had turned a bit of a corner before we did.'

Beth watched the doctor drive off and then turned to walk over to them.

'You know you said you wanted to do something useful?' Michael continued. 'Well, Beth thinks this might be even more useful than antibiotics.' He winked at Beth as she joined them.

'Anything's worth a try Michael so don't knock it just yet. I have here,' and Beth pulled a piece of paper out of her pocket, 'the words of the tree blessing. He needs us to finish it for his peace of mind. Just have a look at it Maeve and keep it with you. We know it, as it's the same one he does

181

every year. I wonder how far he got with it before…?'

'I vaguely remember him saying 'Sacred Spirit' as I reached him. I didn't stop to listen.' said Michael as Beth threw him a look.

'We'll start there then, we won't overlay his former words,' she said.

So Maeve found herself taking part in the second Pagan ritual of the day. She wouldn't tell them about the first as she felt a little silly now but, if it had helped one iota, then she was glad she had done it. It might even turn out to be worth the visit there in more ways than one.

The lightning-struck branch had fallen to the side of the tree and now, as they all held hands, there was enough room for them to move around it. They encircled the Druid's Oak, their bodies almost touching the bark. They walked slowly, stepping carefully over the great roots on the surface of the grass. Beth began and they all joined in.

'Sacred Spirit of the Oak, hear me.
Let your roots be strong and your heart be powerful,
And so give strength to this place.
May your blessings go with us all
To nourish, comfort and sustain us.

182

Let light come into our world.
So May It Be.'

CHAPTER 23

'Wasn't my Tim wonderful?' asked the smitten Carole who, all at once, seemed to have claimed ownership over Tim. 'He picked Ruadhan up and carried him back as if he was no heavier than a child.'

Everyone agreed with her. Maeve struggled to make her mouth do what her brain asked but her mouth won.

'Michael was pretty heroic too, covering Ruadhan's body with his own so he bore the brunt of the branch's weight.'

Out of the corner of her eye, she could see Michael turning slowly towards her with a silly grin on his face. She didn't meet his eyes. Luckily, Beth jumped in.

'He was very brave, even though he's suffering for it now, I'm sure he'd do it again. I'm proud of both of them.'

'And don't forget Maeve, acting as the best-looking walking stick I've ever seen,' Michael said – and this time their eyes met.

'Though of course,' offered Carole who had a tendency to take things at face value, 'Tim makes some beautiful walking sticks too. Yes, it was a good joint effort all round.'

Everyone knew this meant that Tim was still *her* hero. She continued.

'I just hope the idiot will stop going out in the middle of torrential rain and apoth – aploc – apocalyptic storms now, to do his Druid thing.'

'I'm sure he will Carole' smiled Beth. 'For a start, I hope that's the last we see of apocalyptic storms for a long time. And then, we are all here to keep him straight and not let him get in such a perilous state again.'

Carole melted totally.

'You *do* think he'll be all right, don't you?' she sniffed, her eyes watery.

'The doctor was very hopeful,' Beth answered. 'So we should be too.'

At that moment, Tim came into the kitchen.

'Cuppa tea Tim?' asked Carole, brightening up.

'That would be nice,' he smiled.

Tim seemed to have grown in confidence since last night and his attitude towards Carole, once shifting as slowly as the sands of time, had speeded up and become more noticeably softer now.

'He's still sleeping. Hasn't moved since I took over. No better, no worse. Looks peaceful though.'

'Thanks, Tim,' said Beth. 'It's my turn again now. I'm leaving Glenys asleep as she stayed with him before Maeve's shift.'

Beth finished her cup of tea and ate a couple of custard creams as she hadn't been able to face breakfast. As she stood up a few minutes later to go upstairs, she turned to Michael and Maeve.

'Do you want to come up with me to let him know we finished the blessing? There's no telling if he can hear us or not but it might filter through his dreams.'

Maeve remembered Ruadhan saying how spiritual Beth was and she was realising this more than ever now. Upstairs, Rusty met them at the door, his tail wagging and then rushed off down the stairs. This was the first time he had left Ruadhan's side since the accident. He must desperately need food, drink and a trip outside!

All three of them entered his room, creeping as quietly as mice and then realised why Rusty had left his post. They all stopped in their tracks at

Ruadhan trying to sit up whilst also trying to pull the tube from his arm.

'Woah! Don't pull your drip out. Let me help you.'

Michael went over to him and held him forward over his good arm, whilst Maeve pulled the pillows into a slope. Michael laid him back against them. The movement made him cough but – was it Beth's imagination or did it sound better than before?

'Well, you do like to surprise us don't you Ruadhan? First with your impression of Noah defying the floods and now, coming out of a near coma to greet us all.'

Beth smiled as she said this and went over to kiss his cheek so no one could see the tears in her eyes.

'We've been so worried about you,' sniffed Maeve, her own eyes filling up and not caring who saw.

'We've finished your blessing ceremony so now all will be well,' Beth whispered.

'I know,' replied Ruadhan in a ridiculously strong and chirpy voice seeing as he'd been at death's door only hours before. 'I saw you all out there.'

'Please don't tell me you got out of bed,' Michael said in horror.

'I meant I saw you in my dreams. All three of you. And I thank you with all my heart.'

'It's the drugs,' laughed Michael.

'How did he know there were only three of us then?' countered Maeve.

'Because we're here? Telling him?' Michael offered sarcastically.

'And Maeve,' Ruadhan held his hand out to her. 'Thank you for your prayers to Dallhain and the gods in the grove. I know it helped. I could feel my ancestor reach out to me. I could feel it here.'

He patted his heart, making him cough again. Both Beth and Michael gave him a fond smile now.

'Definitely the drugs.' Michael lifted one eyebrow and Beth smiled in agreement. Maeve said nothing as her mouth was wide open and she couldn't shut it. How did he know? The other two had no idea and she wanted to keep it that way, at least for now. It seemed too private. Just between her, Ruadhan and the fairy ring.

'Carole's just made a cup of tea; do you want one? I'll get her to bring it here?' asked Michael.

'I'd love one.'

'And I promised to phone the doctor as soon as you woke up. I'll just fetch my phone. Can you stay with him another minute Maeve?'

'Of course I can' she replied, still in awe of what he'd just said and wondering how she should deal with it. She went over to his side.

'I'm so glad you're okay Ruadhan. There are an awful lot of people who will be happy to hear the news. Since they heard about you, Beth's phone hasn't stopped ringing with everyone asking after you.'

'It's so nice to know that. People are lovely, aren't they?'

'Most are,' admitted Maeve with reservations.

They could hear Beth on the landing, saying something to Carole, so Maeve planted a kiss on Ruadhan's cheek. He whispered to her quickly.

'Don't worry, I won't tell them – but I could feel Dallhain's spirit, his soul, rising in me. I could hear his voice in my head, asking the gods of Nature to heal me. You reached him Maeve. I don't know how but you asked him for help and he answered. Thank you.'

He held her hand and squeezed, weakly still, just as Beth came back in.

Maeve went back to her room thinking, not for the first time, that there was something not quite 'of this world' about Ruadhan. Yet, whatever gods – Nature, God, Spirit, Druidic – she had to thank, the result was the same. Lovely

Ruadhan was back with them and was on the mend.

*

'It's not a bad omen you know,' Ruadhan told Beth as they were waiting for the doctor to arrive. A bit of colour had returned to his cheeks but he was still frail. It even took an effort to lift his arms from the covers to illustrate a point in his conversation. Being a storyteller, he always used his arms expressively. He went on.

'It is a lucky omen. The complete opposite of what you would think, I know. Yet, a piece of wood that has been struck by lightning is believed to be the most powerful talisman available. The lightning-struck tree is empowered by divine forces to provide protection against all harm.'

'It nearly killed you,' Beth looked him in the eyes with only a little rebuke in her tone.

'That's because I was an idiot. I shouldn't have been there.'

'That's two things we can agree on then,' she smiled softly. 'But Ruadhan, the tree might die after the shock. We know it could happen, don't we?'

'It won't, I know that. This oak is stronger than us all put together. Even if that did happen – and it won't - it is the symbolism that matters. The oak represents this place and even if it has been supplanted, the symbol remains. An oak at Druid's Oak Farm.'

'I have saplings growing, as you know, which could be planted if the worst comes to the worst.'

'I have faith that it will survive but the saplings are there for the future. Continuity.'

'And it's really good luck? I thought you would be upset over it.'

'The lightning was a divine messenger. Druid shrines were built where lightning had struck. The gods were honouring those chosen. The power of the lightning passed to the tree – and on to whoever possesses the struck wood.

'It is a renewal. A renewal of this place, its aims, its history. A renewal of the spiritual and creative energy of this place.'

Beth frowned, forming a question in her mind. The question was answered before she could voice it.

'I believe Maeve was the catalyst as, I think, do you? I have felt a difference in the aura of this place since she arrived. It doesn't feel so...defeated any more. I think you must have known this, subconsciously, when you brought her here.'

This took Beth's breath away. The idea hadn't properly formed in her mind but it had been so near the surface.

191

'I think you're right, Ruadhan. As usual.'

He grinned. A watered-down version of his famously, cheerful smile but it was there. Beth would take that, watered-down or not.

'Rusty has been with you throughout. He has been your four-footed nurse. He wouldn't leave you.'

'I know, I felt his presence and he helped me so much, just knowing that he was there with me. All of you too. I am blessed.'

Beth remembered something.

'Maeve has phoned the tree expert that used to visit the estate she worked at. He'll be here in a day or two to look at our oak

'Good. I would like to talk to him.'

'I'll bring him to you.'

'It would be easier if I saw him at the oak, then I could explain–'

Beth squeezed her eyes shut in exasperation.

'Ruadhan!' It was the nearest thing to a shout that Beth could manage. 'For once, you are to do as you are told. Is that understood?'

'Yes mum,' he grinned, taking her hand.

Beth wondered if he would know how much that response had pleased her. She leant forward to plant a kiss on the top of his dear head.

CHAPTER 24

The next day was glorious and the sun shone warmly on the grounds, making a mockery of the fact that, two days earlier, the place could have stood in for the set of a disaster movie.

Everyone was in a good mood because it was becoming obvious that Ruadhan was improving all the time. They were running up and down the stairs with food, drink and good cheer while trying to stop him from coming downstairs and getting back to normal. He wanted to put the finishing touches to his translation of *The Book of Dallhain* but was restrained by being persuaded that he wouldn't give it his full attention just now.

Meanwhile, life went on. Doctor (not medical) Bradborough, a tree specialist, was coming tomorrow to check the Druid's Oak and also, unbeknown to the others, to check out something that Maeve had in mind. She didn't want to get Ruadhan's hopes up just yet.

Today, however, she was driving the wounded invalid into Helmsley. Not Ruadhan but Michael. He'd said he would be quite a while so not to plan on doing any gardening that day. She didn't mind as when she thought back to the night of the storm, Michael would be able to drive himself if he hadn't cared so much for his friend.

He was waiting impatiently by the car he and Beth shared when they couldn't cope with the truck. This wasn't exactly a smooth runner either as it spluttered and coughed its way into life. Not to mention the corrosive rust on the sills. Still, it got them from A to B.

'Am I late?' asked Maeve, ironically.

The rule of this place was that there were no rules and no times so strict that they had to be followed down to the second. However, his face split into a wide grin.

'I just thought you'd forgotten about me,' he said, hangdog look in place as he tried the sympathetic approach. Or just pathetic, thought Maeve.

'Oh god,' she said. 'Just get in the car.'

Michael later disappeared into the streets of Helmsley to places unknown. The art shop was a good guess for a start. Maeve collected Ruadhan's medication from the chemist, who insisted on a complete update on his health.

'He's much better, thank you. Straining at the leash.'

The chemist nodded knowingly, as did everyone else who asked and to whom she trotted out the same stock phrase.

After finishing her errands - more ruled notebooks for Glenys and some sandpaper for Tim - she roamed around the market town. She had hardly brought any clothes with her and they were mostly gardening clothes. She felt like she needed something for 'best'.

There was a small independent clothes shop and surprisingly, once inside, she saw the prices weren't too expensive. She chose a dress which caught her eye, for if ever the occasion allowed it. Not something she was used to wearing, it was figure-hugging at the top but swung out from below the waist. The scooped neckline and the short transparent sleeves marked it out for summer. It was a floral, delicate, floaty creation and she had to admit that she felt special in it.

For the other tops she needed, she visited a charity shop. Her job still didn't pay well and the dress was her one 'splash out' purchase. No one would be able to tell where the tops were from when they were washed and pressed. She rashly kept one of the tops on over her jeans because it smelt better than most of her clothes did. A lavender scent like a clothes conditioner she herself used - up until she had to use the cheap-as-we-can utility wash-powder at the farm. The top was pale yellow with tiny white leaves on it and seemed to reflect the sunny day, although the nearer she got to the car and Michael, the more like a buttercup she felt.

Michael came towards her with a large bag in his right hand. His limp was getting less pronounced.

'Wow, Miss Sunshine,' he said, taking in the bright vision in front of him.

'Too much?' Maeve grimaced.

'It's just a contrast to your gardening clothes, that's all. You look…just right,' he replied earnestly. There were a few seconds of eye contact before Maeve broke it.

'Back to the farm then?' she said.

'Are you in a hurry?'

'No, why?' She sounded belligerent and didn't mean to. The 'just right' comment had thrown her off kilter.

'I thought we might have a picnic? I brought some sandwiches from the bakery, with some fruit for after. And drinks.'

Maeve was thrown once more by his uncharacteristic behaviour. Then again, did she really know him all that well to think it *was* uncharacteristic?

'Oh! Yes, that would be nice. Where?'

'If you get in the car, I'll direct you.'

Maeve did as instructed. Around five minutes later she saw what the destination was. The ruined abbey could be glimpsed along the road and through the trees. Today, the sun shone on the mellow, honey-coloured stone, lighting it up like a beacon of purity. Trees formed a backdrop to the abbey as they burst into life with their vivid, virgin leaves. This, then, was Rievaulx Abbey.

In the car park, she carried the bag of food while Michael got something from the boot. It was a waterproof picnic blanket, essential as the ground was still damp after the soaking it had received. She realised that the blanket hadn't been there when she borrowed the car last week. That meant this wasn't a spur-of-the-moment thing and he had planned it. She started to smile and turned to read the information board so he didn't notice.

The abbey was Cistercian, founded in 1132 but was at its peak thirty years later when its most famous abbot, Abbott Aelred, built most of the buildings still standing today. Aelred was a steward to David 1st of Scotland and came here later, rising through the ranks. He was buried in the east end of the abbey church.

She turned to see Michael waiting for her. After he paid for her, they wandered through into the grounds and she felt the warmth of the Spring sun in this sheltered valley. The monks couldn't have chosen a more picturesque place for their abbey, in a natural hollow with hills to shelter it both from the elements and from enemies. It didn't help when coming up against Henry VIII though.

Maeve drank in the sheer size of the ruins and couldn't fathom what it would have been like in its entirety. To her mind, the ruins were more beautiful and romantic than any original straight lines and angles could have been. The broken edges melted into the natural background as though it was always meant to be that way. And it was peaceful. So peaceful.

She came out of her reverie to find Michael studying her, a bemused expression on his face.

'I thought you were having a religious experience then,' he laughed, wryly.

'You can make fun if you like but it did feel like a profound, spiritual experience. I've been having a lot of those lately,' she added as an afterthought.

Michael gave her a puzzled look.

'Anyway, it does feel like a special, holy place,' she finished.

'That's how you felt about Druid's Oak when you first arrived, isn't it? Without the holy bit?'

'No, this is an experience that I imagine many will feel when they come into contact with Rievaulx. The farm, well, it was more of a personal thing. I felt like I belonged. It felt like it was home.'

'You really are a Romantic, aren't you?'

'You're not?' she asked. She thought she already knew the answer but, after the picnic idea…

'It's not something that has ever been levelled at me, no.'

'Although just bringing me here was a romantic thing to do.' Unfortunately, she spoke the words in her mind, aloud. As soon as they left her mouth, along with the meaning that was inferred, her cheeks coloured up.

'I didn't mean romantic as in me and you. I meant it in the broader sense of romance, (The lady doth protest too much, methinks) as in…well, you know what I mean don't you? (Oh god, I really hope you do).'

'Do I?' He smiled that annoyingly suggestive smile.

'Yes, you do. You're being deliberately obtuse.'

'About what?' he smiled.

'I think I – just got my words muddled up,' she mumbled lamely.

He looked like he was trying to bite back his next words but then suddenly burst out laughing.

'Shut up,' she said decisively, turning to walk towards the ruins.

'Yes ma'am.'

She could picture the big cheesy grin on his face without even turning around to see it.

They found a spot on the grass quite a way behind the ruins, where they could appreciate them in their entirety. If you could call ruins entire. She could see the nave and the arches were mostly intact.

Michael produced a small digital camera from his pocket. Before she knew what was happening, he'd fired off three or four shots of her, probably looking miles away, then startled and then annoyed.

'One more with a smile?'

She duly obliged.

Do you always carry a camera around with you?'

'I do actually, you never know when you might need it. A wonderful sunset or sunrise missed because you left your camera at home. It's not going to happen to me.'

Michael spread the large blanket out on the ground and she handed the sandwiches out. They shared Wensleydale cheese, grated carrot and chutney sandwiches on malted bread - and ham and cheese in soft white breadcakes. Food always tastes better in the open air they say and today, Maeve definitely agreed with that verdict. Every crumb of the sandwiches gone, Michael took a small box of cream cakes out of the bag and offered her first choice.

'Funny looking fruit,' she said.

'There are strawberries in that one. Very healthy,' he replied.

'I think the cream cancels that out.'

'I do have some apples too if you'd rather...' and he started to put the box back in the bag, with exaggeratedly slow movements.

'Bring that back here, Ingram,' she said sternly and picked a cake out quickly.

'Mmm,' she said afterwards. 'That was yummy.'

He didn't answer but just smiled at her. She knew that smile.

'What?' she asked, putting her hand up to her mouth. 'Have I got cream on my face?'

'No,' he answered, still with that smile.

She frowned and then looked down to see a trickle of cream making its way down her chest towards the low scoop neck. It would be in her cleavage any second. She groaned and felt in the bag for one of the paper serviettes, trying not to move.

'You're going to lose it in a minute,' he grinned.

'I can't find a…'

'I can lick it off if you like?'

She stopped breathing.

He moved towards her and she felt his tongue dart out to catch the cream. He sat up again.

'Didn't want it to ruin your new top and it was a shame to waste it,' he said, trying for nonchalance. Yet, Maeve could tell his voice was huskier and his breathing was quicker. She didn't want to admit to herself what it had done to her senses either.

They sat in silence for a few seconds, then gravitated towards each other as though pulled by a magnet. His lips met hers. She closed her eyes and gave herself up to the moment.

CHAPTER 25

Dr Bradborough's car could be seen down the drive and Maeve stepped out to wait for him. He was a non-medical doctor, a tree expert with many years of experience. She was still occupied by yesterday's events at Rievaulx and tried to return her thoughts to trees. Which made her think of the trees at Rievaulx. That kiss. The shyness they both felt afterwards when Maeve thought he was regretting it – before the moment he took her hand to help her over a low wall and kept hold of it right until they reached the car. The smile he gave her when they turned to each other in the car seats, was so gentle. Yet he seemed to have avoided her since, so he might be regretting it? And was she? She certainly wasn't looking for any relationships, especially in this closed community as it would…

'Maeve McQuaid! Hello!'

John Bradborough's voice boomed as he walked towards her, his hand held out. He shook her hand in a vice-like grip. She hadn't noticed the car pull up nearby.

'John, so good to see you. I hope I haven't brought you on a wild goose chase.'

'Giving a talk in Thirsk this evening so it fits in nicely and you know I love any mystery with trees, as well as the obvious problems,' he said, turning to look at the stricken oak.

'If you wouldn't mind looking at that first?' she asked. 'Unless you want a cup of tea while we discuss your fees?'

'Are you feeding me?' John was huge in height and his girth was slowly filling out too. He was known for his love of food.

'We are and Carole is a good cook. She has made a chicken and ham pie in your honour if that's okay? Not too heavy for lunchtime?' She knew the answer already.

'That sounds just up my street – and will do for payment, as well as unlimited mugs of tea of course. A favour for a friend and – I've always wanted to see this famous oak, so you're doing me a favour too.'

'You're a star but I hope it's not too damaged. I hope it is salvageable.'

He looked across at the tree and frowned.

'I'll have to get a closer look of course. How about we have that cup of tea first and you introduce me to Ruadhan?'

*

In the end, he had spent half an hour talking to Ruadhan as they got on famously. Beth managed to persuade the recovering patient to sit still, wrapped up warmly, in a chair in front of the house to watch proceedings, which made it a little awkward for what Maeve had planned for after. John, who knew the situation, said he would go in for lunch and persuade Ruadhan to rest a little and then she and John could slip out.

John now moved swiftly, watched by Ruadhan's eagle eye. He borrowed Billy's ladders and took samples from further up where the branch had torn off and then examined the branch itself. He moved backwards and forwards with various instruments. He extracted an increment core sample from the tree with a borer and examined the trunk of the tree closely. After all this and because Ruadhan had asked him to, he measured the circumference and then divided it by 2.5. Then he measured the height of the tree. He stood with his back to the tree and with legs apart and straight, he bent down to look at the tree through his legs. Then he hobbled forward until he could see the very top of the tree through his legs.

Standing straight, he then measured the distance from where he was to the tree.

By the time John was shuffling forward, looking between his legs, Maeve was in hysterics. She turned towards Beth who was also laughing. Even Tim had come out from the barn to grin at the antics of this strange man.

'That can't be a legitimate method, surely?' Maeve laughed as he wrote the measurements in his notebook.

'It most certainly is, young lady. Would you prefer I shinned up to the top of the tree with a tape measure?'

'No, I wouldn't want you to do that without your hard hat and your safety harness, most definitely.'

She had seen him at the top of a massive Copper Beech at Sigwardby Estate and just the sight of it had given her vertigo.

After another quick inspection of the oak, they walked over to Beth and Ruadhan before going inside for lunch. Ruadhan just had soup but the others tucked into the huge pie Carole had made. John made appreciative noises and when he told Carole that it was the best pie he'd ever tasted, she looked like she was going to burst with pride.

Over a pot of tea, John gave his findings to the four of them.

'I can't say anything for definite before I analyse the core sample but – from my other observations I would say that the Druid's Oak has a very good chance of surviving.'

There was a collective sigh of relief but Ruadhan looked like he had already taken this fact for granted. John went on.

'As you no doubt know, Ruadhan, oak trees get hit by lightning more than most other trees. The lightning can strike right through the middle of the tree, splitting it and causing irreparable tissue damage. If however – and I think it is the case with your tree – the bark is soaked through with rain, the lightning travels only through the bark, sparing the inner tree.

'I would even go as far as to say that the lower branch, the one that was struck, was already weakened with the start of disease and it is almost providence that it was sliced off before it could get worse and infect the whole tree. It is probably the reason that the lightning travelled down through the bark and found its weakness there, instead of further up. You must clean the 'wound' as it can be infected with fungi or pests if left. Apart from that, I am hoping that this magnificent tree will carry on for another four hundred years.'

'Is that how old it is?' asked Ruadhan. 'I already knew it wasn't the original that my ancestor mentioned but it could have been on the same spot?'

'Possibly,' said John, giving Maeve a swift glance. 'Yes, the tree is – and I can't be any more accurate at the moment – between four and five hundred years old.'

'That would tie in with it being planted – or replaced,' Beth said for Ruadhan's benefit, 'when the Elizabethan hall was first built. Around 1572?'

'About four hundred and fifty years old that would make it? Yes, smack bang in the middle. Did you know, Ruadhan, that when an oak is struck by lightning, it becomes particularly sacred and powerful? Talismans were made of lightning-struck wood as they had been 'touched by the gods''

'I have been saying that very thing, John,' Ruadhan smiled. 'Perhaps they will believe me now that a tree expert has told them.'

'I didn't think you believed in things like that John,' Maeve said in surprise.

'You can't devote your life to trees and their life and history, without believing the lore surrounding them. Sometimes, science is not the only answer.'

Ruadhan nodded wisely.

'And now, before I go, Maeve and I are going to catch up with the news while we walk around the grounds. I will come and say goodbye before I go.'

*

John mentioned on the way down that, if this Great oak wasn't the original oak, it had probably been placed more or less in the middle of the grass area instead, so as to be more aesthetically pleasing. It would also have been easier to access for the many villagers who danced around it and used it for their Pagan festivals since the late fifteen hundreds or early sixteen hundreds.

As soon as Maeve and John had reached the clearing, he could see clearly what was laid out before him.

'You were right Maeve. The darker ring of grass means that there is a hole or disturbed soil underneath and the fairy ring of mushrooms – or as we still like to call them, toadstools – indicates wood that has rotted down in the earth below it. The size of the ring would suggest a large tree - *and* rotted oaks are the trees where it is most common for toadstools to appear.'

'I knew it!' shouted an exultant Maeve.

'Although I think you're right about there originally being a central oak in the Druid Grove, I can't say for certain, so don't get Ruadhan's hopes up just yet. However, I am quite happy for you to say that it is *possible* for his ancestor's remains to be buried here, just as long as he knows it is just as possible that there is nothing at all.'

'I promise John. I will tell him exactly what you have told me. I really can't thank you enough. Both for the Druid's Oak – and possibly the original Druid's Oak too!'

'Now, I must get to my hotel in Thirsk and get a shower so I can have my dinner before the talk.'

'Your second dinner?' she laughed.

'I'm a growing lad!' he grinned

*

There was a silence. Maeve could almost see the cogs turning in Ruadhan's brain.

'You mean that–'

'I don't mean anything because I'm not sure of anything. Please remember what John said. It's only a vague possibility that Dallhain is buried under what was probably an oak in the clearing. Neither of us wanted to get your hopes up for you to be disappointed.'

'But, *you* think he's there. You had a feeling?'

'I didn't say that Ruadhan,' although he was right, she had. She was just worried that she had set wheels in motion that should have been left alone.

'That's why we both had a feeling about that place. Why it seemed special. I can't believe I didn't think of it before.'

'You're not a tree expert Ruadhan and neither am I of course but I'd seen something similar when I worked at the estate. How could you know?'

'Kit!' Ruadhan yelled. He was getting back to full strength now but was still being told to take it steady, which didn't sit well with him. His eyes were glassy with excitement now.

'Kit Courtney,' he continued. The man I met when I did my ancient history course at York. He's a professor of archaeology. He did the dig I helped with on Winterside Howe.'

The name which had seemed familiar now sprung to life in Maeve's mind.

'Do you think he'll take a look?' she asked.

'If he's not too busy, I think his interest will be piqued. He knew about Dallhain and even did a few test boreholes in the soil around the Druid's Oak but couldn't find a disturbance of soil or any difference in the grade of soil. I'll ring him tonight. I stayed with him and his wife Annie in Winterfell in the Yorkshire Dales, just before I asked Beth if I could live here. I count him as a friend.'

'Pleeeease don't get too excited Ruadhan, I'll feel terrible if…'

'Maeve,' he said, coming across to hug her. 'I won't – but it is worth a try. If there are no remains there, then I am no worse off than I am now. I just think it's so nice of you to think of me. I know I get a bit obsessed with the history of my ancestors.'

'I just want to help if I can,' she said, hoping she wasn't making things worse. 'It was when I was praying to Dallhain and his gods for you to get better, that the significance of the toadstool fairy ring hit me.'

'Almost like fate, wouldn't you say?' Ruadhan smiled, knowingly.

Maeve sighed. Well, they would soon find out one way or another. Michael poked his head around the door.

'I've just walked from the fairy ring to the house. Ignoring all the trees in the wood, I traced a straight line up to the main door of the farm. I thought it might interest you to know that, as Dallhain said in his manuscript, he wanted to be buried under the Great Oak, which was in a direct line with the door. It makes even more sense now that the Great Oak he was talking about was the one under the fairy ring and not the one set off to the side.'

Ruadhan took this in slowly then grabbed the phone as Maeve looked at Michael with a 'You've done it now' expression on her face. The next minute, Ruadhan spoke.

'Hello, is that you Kit? It's Ruadhan.'

CHAPTER 26

Kit Courtney had been excited by the news. He had been disappointed by his cursory examination under the Great Oak tree, years earlier. He knew that the area around the farm was of historical interest and not just because of the Winterside Howe burial mound he'd excavated but because of the earlier Great Hall and the eighth-century manuscripts Ruadhan had translated into modern English.

He had offered to come over first thing on Saturday morning as he would be lecturing on Friday at the University of York but Beth immediately asked him to stay at the farm on Friday night after the lecture to save him staying in a hotel.

Maeve had found Kit easy to get on with, if obsessed with history and archaeology. No wonder he got on so well with Ruadhan. Carole obviously found him attractive as Maeve noticed how she fluttered around him and drank in his compliments on her food as though it was manna from heaven.

Maeve was also amused to see that Tim was jealous. He had returned to his 'grumpy Tim' persona that he had been slowly but steadily emerging from. He glowered when Carole giggled at something Kit said and he was obviously put out that he had been pushed into second place by this interloper even though he knew Kit was a very happily married man.

Privately, Maeve thought it served him damn well right for ignoring Carole's overtures for so long, then immediately thought this was uncharitable. Tim had trust issues on top of his innate shyness and he was never going to rush headlong into any relationship. Besides, she had noticed Carole's sly little glances in Tim's direction after any interaction between her and Kit. Tim was being played like a fiddle by Carole – and good luck to her, thought Maeve.

Kit and Ruadhan were down at the clearing at the moment. They had gone down just after breakfast. Michael had ten people coming for a photographic shoot of the stricken oak – never one to miss an opportunity, he had said – but he went with them for now. Maeve helped Beth clear up as

Carole and Tim eyed each other, the former with amusement, the latter with suspicion.

Glenys put the kettle on again for a coffee and then went to prepare for her next poetry session on Sunday. The difference in her since she had started the poetry days had been palpable. Her tutoring at the college had a wage attached to it too, which made her feel like she was pulling her weight. Both activities had given Glenys her pride back. She had invited Maeve to one of the poetry sessions in the dining room – 'Keats – Love and Tragedy' – and she had seen a different Glenys. In command and enjoying herself, Maeve could see what a good teacher she would have been.

Beth had been telling Maeve how much she enjoyed the meditation and yoga sessions, even though she had only had two so far. It was nice to connect with the outside world she said, as they had become very 'cut off'. There were only she and Beth left in the kitchen now so they took their coffees into the Elizabethan garden to sit on a bench in the sun. More flowers were coming out every day and most of the residents came and sat there in contemplation with a hot drink at least once a day. Another joint open day with Bert had been held last week. It had been a success but Maeve knew it was still a work in progress.

They heard Bert's old pick-up rumble to life as he went to collect something from Helmsley. This reminded Maeve of her suspicions regarding Glenys and Bert. She told Beth that if only they would get together, it would seal Glenys's happiness. Beth looked puzzled so she explained about the encounter between Glenys and Bert in the greenhouse and how she had linked it to Glenys's poem that she had seen, with the mysterious 'G'. Now Maeve knew his name was Gilbert, it was the only possible solution.

This didn't have the effect she thought it would have on Beth. Beth the all-knowing. Beth the empath. Surely she would have guessed the link before now, thought Maeve? Beth stopped the mug halfway to her lips, then stared into it for a very long minute, during which time, Maeve thought she'd overstepped the mark. When Beth finally took a sip of the coffee, Maeve realised she had been holding her own breath.

'It's very nice of you to worry about Glenys's romantic life Maeve but perhaps we shouldn't speculate.'

This was the nearest she had come to a rebuke from Beth and she felt suitably chastened and a little upset, like a child who knows she has somehow displeased her mother but isn't sure why.

'Oh, I'm so sorry. I wasn't going to interfere. I just thought that it would be nice for both of them if they–'

A loud sigh had escaped from Beth which stopped Maeve mid-sentence. She watched the older woman take another sip of her coffee and then turn to face her with what looked like resignation.

'Maeve, this is not my story to tell but before you do or say anything you will regret, listen to me. I know you well and I trust you, so I know this will go no further.'

Maeve nodded, feeling confused.

'The 'G' you and Glenys were referring to wasn't Bert. Bert was very much in love with his wife. When she died, he was devastated. His work here keeps him busy and he has rebuilt his life since but there is no room in that life for another partner.

'He and Glenys get on as friends. Perhaps they both recognise that they have both lost people they loved and the agony this brings. Perhaps they have even talked about it and it has created a bond. Yet I don't believe either of them wants another relationship but are just content to have friends they can talk to.'

Maeve still persisted, like a runaway train.

'But, don't you think it would be nice for them if they *did* get together?'

Beth put her coffee down beside her on the bench and steepled her hands together before smiling indulgently at Maeve.

'You are young. You like happy endings, endings that can be tied up with a big bow and labelled romance. I love that about you and want you to keep it, as life has a very good chance of working out that way. But, there are other ways of life too, a life that can be happy without the need for a partner.

'The 'G' of Glenys's poem was another teacher at the school where they both taught. The rejection she received in a particularly cruel manner was the reason she left and the reason for her breakdown. That 'G' was another woman.'

'Oh,' whispered Maeve, unable to say anything else.

'Glenys is quite happy here as she is. I know sometimes she doesn't appear to be but that's just her character. She is content – and may I say – much more so after you forced her to go back to her first love, Poetry and English literature. She is the happiest now that I have ever seen her. So, please, don't worry about her, although I can understand why you did and it is because you have a kind heart. I worry about all my little family but

219

I'm sure, if push came to shove, that they would all be able to stand on their own two feet.'

Maeve put her head in her hands and groaned.

'What an idiot I am! I crash into situations without giving them a minute's thought first.'

A pause, then.

'I feel like Jane Austen's Emma, getting my matchmaking so horribly wrong.'

Beth laughed and touched Maeve's hand. Maeve looked at Beth with a smile then frowned. She tried to rein herself in but her voice manifested itself before her brain caught up. It was that mention of Beth's 'family' again.

'What's your story, Beth? I mean you and your brother started this artistic community but…'

Maeve swallowed hard. Was she trying to get all the secrets prised out of Beth before she was finally cast out of the heaven that was Druid's Oak Farm for interfering? She knew she should leave well alone but her voice carried on as though it were a separate entity.

'…but was it at the expense of your personal life? I mean,' Maeve faltered, 'you've never married.'

She felt so disloyal saying these things to Beth but conversely, because she felt so close to her, she wanted to know her story. The story that this private person had kept from her. Maeve felt like she wouldn't truly belong here if there were secrets between them. Maeve herself was an open book but she realised she had lived here less than three months. What right did she have? It *was* Beth's story to tell and she had chosen not to tell her. She should have respected that and now, as the silence dragged on, she jumped up from the bench, mumbling her apologies. The next moment she felt Beth catch hold of her hand and pull her gently back down to the bench. She kissed Maeve's cheek and smiled.

'It's alright Maeve, I'm happy to tell you. The occasion never arose but I was always going to tell you at some point. You are part of my family now, the family I never had.

'I met my partner not long after Ned and I started this place. Karim had just come for a visit while he was on a tour of Britain. He came for a day and stayed for fifteen years. He was a sculptor and contributed financially and aesthetically to this place. He was one of our most successful residents.'

'The marble bust in the sitting room!' Maeve burst out.

'It's wonderful, isn't it? He was so talented.' She paused, her mind elsewhere, before continuing.

'We fell in love immediately. We were incredibly happy together. We lived here together for almost the whole fifteen years. We never had children; it just didn't happen. We didn't know if it was Karim or me and we decided not to investigate. It didn't matter. If nature had dealt us that hand then we were just as happy in each other's company, if that was meant to be.

'Unfortunately, he became ill. Lung cancer. Those god-awful roll-ups he used to smoke before any of us realised how bad smoking was. He died here, surrounded by the people he loved. He was holding my hand as he went.'

Tears had started to trickle down Maeve's cheeks and she didn't realise until Beth wiped them away.

'Don't be sad, please. We enjoyed the years we had together and we were so happy. Most people never get that sort of love in their lives at all, so I count myself lucky. So... when I call you my family, I mean it. Not particularly my substitute children but the people who mean the most to me in this life. The people who come together when it matters, like cooperating on the open days you started and as on the night of the storm. The people who I can trust with my life. You are all my family now.'

Maeve gave her a tear-soaked smile. This strong woman, this compassionate woman, was someone that she admired and, yes, loved. She put her arms around her and they stayed that way for a while until they heard the kitchen door open and Michael appeared.

'I think you'd better come to the clearing,' he said and on seeing their worried expressions, clarified. 'Ruadhan is fine but you need to hear what Kit has to say.'

CHAPTER 27

What Kit had to say proved very interesting indeed and set everything in motion.

For the past couple of weeks, the clearing near the sacred pool had been occupied by Kit, two post-graduate students from his archaeology course, an ever-present Ruadhan, sundry farm residents and Rusty, who had been banished - haughty expression on his face - to the edge of the clearing under the silver birches, to keep him away from the excavation site. Ruadhan was just a fidgety observer at first but as he got stronger, he had joined in. Now he was fully recovered and was more in danger of keeling over from sheer excitement than any lingering illness.

Kit had brought his metal detector at the beginning. He had discovered that the detector was sending out a strong reading, over 14kHz –

whatever that meant - strong enough to suggest a good deposit of gold underneath the fairy ring.

Maeve had been surprised, both at the suggestion of gold when they were only searching for human remains and at the use of a metal detector. She thought that metal detectorists and archaeologists were mortal enemies. Kit told her that times had moved on and unless the detectorists were nighthawks – illegal treasure hunters – then metal detectors, along with geophysics, had a valid part to play in archaeology today.

Kit had delayed another dig up in Scotland to fit this one in as he had a feeling that it could be an important one. It would only be a small dig as there was no evidence of any building here. His natural curiosity and archaeologist's instinct made him sure he was doing the right thing. That and Ruadhan's unshakeable belief that Dallhain lay here under the soil.

Ruadhan himself had uncovered, nearly a week later, what were thought to be his ancestor's remains. The pottery urn indicated the right time period and all the residents and workers at Druid's Oak gathered around. There was complete silence as Ruadhan finally, after yet more careful brushing and scraping of the earth around it, had lifted out the almost intact urn containing Dallhain's ashes.

They were revealed through the side of the urn where a shard had broken off.

Tears sprang to his eyes as he told them all of his absolute conviction that this was Dallhain. He also credited Maeve with knowing this before he did but, as she tried to explain, it was only because he had a 'feeling' here, that she had the idea in the first place.

Maeve was surprised to see that they weren't just ashes. There were bone parts, including smaller splinters, that had been damaged and reduced in the burning process. This was apparently normal at the time. Kit was especially happy with the fragments as it was now possible to be in with a good chance of telling the age and sex of the remains. The grave goods had already indicated a male.

After much careful extraction of the artefacts, cleaning them slowly and painstakingly, photographing, drawing and cataloguing them all, they were now here on display for everyone to see. They had been using Tim's barn to clean and sort everything and the finds were all on a long pine table dragged from the side, all labelled with dates, purpose and possible history. There were three objects in particular that everyone wanted to see in their cleaned-up forms. The same objects that had to be stored in Beth's locked cupboard in the house.

Today, the farm residents queued up to see all the finds and Kit was on hand to tell them any history he and Ruadhan had found out. Maeve and Michael moved along the table together, in awe of what they were seeing. Among the lesser finds was a silver broad penny from the early seven hundreds. It was found amongst Dallhain's ashes as it had probably been placed under his tongue after death, This was meant to pay his way in the afterlife. There was also a plain iron knife. Kit said that the lack of any further weaponry showed the man wasn't a warrior.

The next object of importance was a bronze ring brooch, pin still attached, which would have been used to fasten Dallhain's cloak together. The next object - and here, she could feel Michael's hands squeezing her shoulders in anticipation – was a gold arm Torq, often worn by Druids. They moved along the table, silent now. Kit stood behind the table next to two objects, ready and willing to give any explanation if needed. The find that had excited Ruadhan almost as much as the remains was next up. The man himself jumped up.

'You see,' he gabbled animatedly, 'I always thought that when Dallhain said he wanted to be buried with his Ogham talisman under the oak,

227

that the talisman was made of wood and would probably have perished. But here – look! The talisman, worn round his neck on a leather cord, was pure gold! And see here too, the Ogham marking on it. It is the Ogham equivalent of D, which could have stood for Dallhain. Yet the meaning of that same Ogham mark is also Oak. The tree of the Druids.'

Ruadhan was hopping about like a bunny in Spring.

'Don't you just love it when a plan comes together' whispered Michael in her ear.

'Ruadhan, it's all fantastic! I just can't believe it,' Maeve grinned.

'And all down to you Maeve,' he beamed back.

'Rubbish,' she said. 'You were directing operations from your trance-like state in your sick bed whilst kidding everyone you were asleep.'

'I did see you there, didn't I?' he laughed, pleased with himself too. He looked down at the gold pendant. 'It's a shame that it can't be placed back in the grave when we rebury Dallhain. I feel bad that his cherished talisman can't go with him.'

Ruadhan's smile dropped a little.

'We discussed this Ruadhan, and we came up with an alternative,' said Michael, gently.

'Oh, and it's an excellent idea!' Ruadhan bounced back immediately. 'In fact, the more I think of it, the more I know Dallhain would approve as much as I do.'

Kit joined in.

'You know that these finds are too important to be buried again – apart from the urn and ashes. We need to return those to his resting place. I know Beth wanted it all to go to the local museum at Malton but these finds are so important that they need to be displayed at the British Museum for now.'

Beth, standing at the end of the table, reluctantly nodded.

'I know it's the sensible thing to do. At least everyone from Hawbury will be able to see them here on May Day before they go. And yes, I will keep them safely locked away for two days until then,' she smiled, rightly guessing that Kit would mention it. He grinned.

'But the main reason for the security – and for all the excitement is this…' and he pointed down to the object in front of him on the table.

The pectoral cross, large and solid gold, was set with garnets, pearls and blue glass. It was not only the monetary value of the cross, which was considerable – but the cross could be proved to belong to King Ceolwulf of Northumbria. In

Dallhain's manuscript, he had mentioned the king, now no longer king but living a holy life at Lindisfarne, visiting his former lodge and employees several times to try and convert them to Christianity. Ceolwulf seemed to accept that their lives were too firmly rooted in 'Paganism', especially Dallhain. His bard had mentioned the holy cross his king wore around his neck and described it in detail. It was the same cross that lay in front of them now. Kit spoke again.

'It seemed quite a cruel thing for Ceolwulf to do, putting a Christian cross in the grave of a committed Pagan. Yet it was obvious from *The Book of Dallhain,* which was dedicated to the king, that he was very close to his favourite bard and counted him as a friend. He would not have dishonoured him. It almost seemed like he thought he was saving Dallhain's soul by the act of leaving his own cross with him.

'As we have the written evidence that this cross belonged to King Ceolwulf, it is counted as proof positive. I would hazard a guess that the gold ogham pendant was a gift from him too in the years before he left for the monastery. Perhaps he even gave him the cross before Dallhain died and not as a funerary offering? We can only conjecture but…' Kit turned to Beth, 'I think you can honestly stop worrying about repairing your farm,

Beth. I would be very surprised if these finds bring you less than two million pounds.'

He had told them this before but they still could hardly believe it.

'So, how long between Beth offering the hoard to the British Museum and the Crown paying her the full value?' asked Michael.

'Well, you know these things aren't instant and there's still a lot of investigation to be done because people like to draw these things out as long as they possibly can...' Kit lifted his eyebrows.

'It's just that,' Michael began, then looked across at Billy and Tim 'We have the paint and we have a lot of pledges from the people of Hawbury who would like to help paint the outside.'

'Pledges, paint?' Beth's head swivelled. 'What's this?'

'You've no idea how fond the local people are of you Beth,' Michael explained. 'I bought the paint earlier so the Winterhill Howe money didn't go on less important things, and loads of people offered to help. We were just waiting until after May Day and warmer weather. It seems a bit redundant now this has happened. We should maybe wait for the thatch to be done first – but at least you have the paint at Bert's for when you need it.'

'Oh Michael, that's so kind of you and all of our friends here too,' she looked around at everyone gathered there – 'and all the village. I will thank them on May Day with a day they won't forget. That will just be for the thought, though, not the work, which they won't have to do now. We've waited this long, I'm sure we can wait a bit longer to finally get this place repaired. The thatch, the outside of the house, the window frames and especially the squeaky, creaky, clanking plumbing and heating that ought to be on this table as domestic antiquities'

CHAPTER 28

Rusty had, for once, deserted Ruadhan and turned his attention back to Beth. It was almost as if he knew that Ruadhan was well again and didn't need the constant vigilance of his four-legged nurse. Beth was sure that Rusty had helped his recovery and Ruadhan was one hundred percent certain that he had - along with Maeve's visit to the fairy ring.

Right now, Rusty was leaning against Beth's legs in the kitchen. If she moved, he would fall over in a heap. She laughed at him and stroked the top of his head, as she thought about everything that had happened. It was almost unbelievable. Could it be karma? Good things come to those who either wait or at least don't disrupt the universe too much? Meeting Maeve was the catalyst that set it all in motion, she felt sure of it, although Maeve herself was ignorant of this and would be too modest to accept it as a possibility anyway.

Everyone at Druid's Oak seemed happier now.

Glenys had started to have long conversations with both her and Maeve on books, poems, the arts and well, anything under the sun. Even Michael had a short conversation thrown at him, like a dog biscuit, every now and again. He was bemused but inwardly pleased, she was sure.

Tim had come on in leaps and bounds since the awful night of the storm. He seemed to have grown in confidence and had started to accept – and even enjoy – Carole's devotion, which was stronger now than ever. He had the idea of using the good parts of the stricken branch to help repair the farm doors, to build the good luck in with it. He was also making them each a small memento out of it so they would never forget that day.

Michael…she smiled to herself. He had trust issues from his parents and from an earlier bad relationship of his own. He had been on his own for too long and had thrown himself into the solitary occupation of painting. Yet he and Maeve had an attraction between them, although they both tried very hard to hide it from each other and everyone else too. Maeve had also been let down in her relationship before she came here, so here they were, both pussy-footing around each other. Beth knew it would all work out in the end, she could feel it in her bones.

Maeve hadn't changed much – and didn't need to. She was still the same basically happy, enthusiastic, creative person she had probably been all her life. At last here though, she had room to grow.

Ruadhan. The same fond smile again as she thought of him. His longed-for hope of finding his bardic ancestor had finally come true. Even if this hadn't happened, it would have been enough for him to live in the same place Dallhain had lived. His love of history was kindled by this place. It was steeped in history. Whether it was the Winterside Howe warrior or the King and the Druid: Whether it was the Elizabethan house built on the bones of the Anglo-Saxon Great Hall or whether it was the traditions of hundreds of years of celebrations around Druid's Oak to celebrate the Pagan year. All of it intrigued him. Like everyone here, he had found his spiritual home.

As for herself, she was more content now than she had been in a long while. She had despaired of the money situation and the torpor that everyone had settled into. Even a bracing trek along the Yorkshire Coast when she met Maeve hadn't dispelled those thoughts. She had felt herself slipping into a hole where there was no way out. Now, she had her family back and life was wonderful again.

After everything had settled down and before the work on the house began, she was going to treat herself to that holiday in the Orkneys, to see the great, five-thousand-year-old stones of the Ring of Brodgar and Skara Brae too. She didn't need the yoga and meditation that she had been using as a prop recently but she could never give it up. It was part of her now and, thanks to Maeve, she was helping other people discover the inner peace it could bring.

Carole bounced in through the hall doorway to the kitchen. She had moved into her own rooms at the farm on a permanent basis after the storm, as she became closer to Tim. There was only a salad for dinner tonight as the reburial service was later on so it was easier. Besides, the weather this last week had been so hot it was almost a heatwave. In the grove for the last days of the dig, they had been sheltered from the direct heat of the sun but it was still uncomfortably warm. May 1st was living up to its old function as the first traditional day of Summer at the halfway point between the Spring equinox and the Summer solstice.

Beth got up from her chair without thinking and, true to form, Rusty keeled over into an undignified heap, back paws stuck up in the air. He managed to look both surprised and offended at the same time. Beth laughed – would he never learn? She could hear the others arriving for dinner, clattering down the stairs or coming in from the garden. She had something she needed to ask them but it would wait until after their meal.

*

'I don't know if any of you noticed but we had a visitor this afternoon?

Beth had asked everyone to stay behind before they got ready for the ceremony. They all looked at her anxiously.

'No, nothing wrong at all. I just wanted your opinion. This is a close community and I think decisions should be made between us, don't you?'

'You have always consulted us, Beth,' said Michael. 'Even when you invited Maeve over. We all knew about it - so nothing has changed there. Who was the visitor?'

'Dr Ardley,' she answered. The faces, which had relaxed only a moment before, now looked even more uneasy.

'Are you all right?' asked Ruadhan, his face a mask of concern.

'Yes, perfectly. He wasn't here in his official capacity. You know he retires from his practice very soon. He has reached that age but also, the times now are not the same as they were, they have moved on and left him behind.'

'An excellent doctor, nevertheless,' added Ruadhan. Dr Ardley was another to whom he felt he owed his life.

'He is, none better- but that doesn't mean as much as it once did, in his eyes. But – he came here to ask me something that had been on his mind for a few years now.'

Maeve and Carole both looked at each other with raised eyebrows and a grin. They had mentioned about his fondness for Beth before.

'No, not that, you can put any thoughts of that nature out of your minds right now' Beth said sternly but with her eyes still registering amusement.

'He says he has loved the idea of our creative, artistic community at the farm for as long as he can remember and, as retirement beckoned, he thought more and more about how much he'd like to live here. He wants to write in peace in the countryside instead of in a room overlooking a busy road.'

'He writes?' asked Michael. 'What sort of things?'

'Gory crime novels – he told my dad,' laughed Carole.

'So,' continued Beth, if you all agree – and I told him I'd ask you first – then he'll rent his house out in Helmsley and pay me rent for his rooms.'

They all looked around at each other but from their expressions, they seemed to be in general agreement. 'Fine by me' was the consensus.

'It will be nice to have someone else here to expand our family. Maeve has made such a difference to us since she arrived.'

This little gem came from such an unexpected source that they all went quiet with shock. Glenys, whose words they were, looked a little confused.

'Don't you agree?' she asked, looking unsure now.

'Oh we do Glenys,' laughed Michael. 'It's something I'm unaccustomed to but - yes, I definitely agree with you.'

Glenys tutted at him with an indulgent smile, as Maeve went over and gave her a hug. Glenys tried not to look pleased at this but ended up beaming as Michael kissed the top of her head and Tim patted her on the pack. Beth mentally hugged herself, how times had changed - and so quickly.

'So, if we're happy about it, I'll tell him tomorrow when he comes up for the May Day celebrations.'

They all went out of the kitchen, chatting about the latest developments but when they got into the hall, Michael grabbed Maeve's hand.

'Come and see my etchings,' he whispered to her.

*

The touch of his hand did strange things to her nerve endings but she wondered why he was bringing her here. They hadn't got long to get ready for the Beltane ceremony at the grove. He closed the studio door behind them and led her over towards the window, where a large canvas was covered by a linen cloth.

'Now don't get angry with me,' he began.

Maeve frowned.

'Why would I be angry?' she asked.

'I'm not sure. Invasion of privacy? One never knows with you.' He looked less confident than she'd ever seen him.

Invasion of *privacy?* Maeve had an awful vision of herself in the nude on a giant canvas.

'Come over here,' he said, beckoning her over to stand in front of the canvas, as he slowly pulled the cover off.

Maeve gasped and then stared in amazement, unable to drag her eyes from the painting. She recognised the enigmatic smile and the wild, red hair tumbling over her shoulders from the photograph he had taken of her at the Rievaulx Abbey picnic. She had been looking over at the ruins with a faraway look in her eyes. The rest though, wasn't the same.

She was wearing a long white robe which seemed insubstantial, almost made of smoke and air. She had a garland of white flowers and green leaves in her hair. She was standing against the Druid's Oak before it had been struck by lightning, her eyes gazing into the distance, dreamy, ethereal.

The tree and the surroundings were painted in his trademark style, not quite photographic but recognisable. Leaves were blowing past in the background, moved by a gentle breeze and in the foreground, tiny parts of dandelion clocks and blossom petals floated around her and the tree. Light came down through the tree, the sun's rays highlighting her face and hair - and pinpricks of light floated around her. At her feet, enclosing both her and the tree, was a fairy ring.

Minutes passed, or so it seemed, until Michael finally spoke.

'Oh god Maeve, say something! Even if it's only that you hate it. It's not knowing that's killing me.'

She came out of her dream, the dream that was echoed in the painting before her. She turned to him.

'Michael, it's beautiful.' She turned to it again and was lost in it before she realised. Once more, she made an effort to come back to the moment.

'I love your paintings. They're magical. So real you could reach out and touch the things in it but at the same time, almost of another world. They transport you.'

He sighed with obvious relief.

'I was going to keep it just for me but it's yours if you want it? If you don't. I thought Beth might like it. I'd like it to stay at the farm.'

'So would I,' she answered. 'It belongs here, so if Beth would like it, that would be perfect. I can't believe how beautiful you have made it.'

'You belong here too,' he said, 'as do I. I know that now. Maeve, you are beautiful. So beautiful.'

He pulled her towards him and tracked her cheek with his thumb. He looked into her eyes, his own unfocused and hazy with longing.

Then he kissed her.

CHAPTER 29

<u>Beltane – May Eve</u>

Like All Hallows' Eve, Beltane was a time of year when the veil between the worlds of dark and light was thinnest. As they were coming into the light, the whole celebration was more light-hearted. Fairies and sprites instead of witches and hobgoblins.

Beltane was traditionally celebrated from sunset on April 30th to sunset on May 1st. The evening of April 30th was known in some countries as Walpurgis night but around here, it was simply May Eve.

At the farm, they watched as the sun started its descent to the flat top of Winterside Hill. A procession, led by Ruadhan, walked slowly from the farm. Those at the front carried lighted torches. Towards the back, Carole carried a box of food under one arm and a wooden crate with a carrying handle in her other hand, that was filled with bottles of mead and glasses. Bringing up the rear whilst trying to avoid tripping over Rusty's paws, was Glenys. She carried the torch stakes and a pile of blankets. Rusty had his eyes on the food box and nothing else.

The sky was blazing red above the hill, just turning to a deeper purple on the edges of solid land. In the clearing - the Druid's Grove – the colour was sprinkled and kaleidoscoped throughout the silver birches - darting and dancing like will o' the wisps between the fledgling leaves and onto the ground, almost as if the trees were a natural form of sun-catcher, spreading their light.

Maeve caught her breath. Not just at the beauty of it but because it looked so much like the magical effect of Michael's paintings that it couldn't be a coincidence. She turned to him in astonishment and he gave her a knowing smile and the faintest of nods.

There was a bowl placed nearby and, in the centre where a hole at least four feet by four feet had been left, stood two objects. One was the urn containing Dallhain's ashes. The other was one of the saplings that Bert had grown from a Druid's Oak acorn.

They all remained standing around the grave after Michael and Tim placed all the torches in their stakes. Ruadhan stood at the head of the grave.

'I want to thank you all for being with me today and sharing this precious goodbye with me. He is important to us all and his soul lives on in this blessed place- and in me. Would you, Michael…?'

Michael helped him to lift the heavy urn as Tim stepped forward. As Ruadhan thanked him, Tim placed an oak pendant on a leather cord – an exact copy of Dallhain's original gold talisman, inside the urn. The same symbol was engraved on it. It was made by Tim from the lightning-struck branch, which would grant the remains a safe passage to the afterlife once again.

They lowered it slowly towards its final resting place and put a thick covering of soil over it. Then Ruadhan picked up the oak sapling.

'Maeve, come and help me with this?' he asked.

Maeve went over to pick up the spade leaning against one of the trees and while Ruadhan held the sapling in place, Maeve lifted the rest of the soil until it was almost, but not quite, covering the top roots.

Carole had asked earlier if the roots would grow through the ashes. Ruadhan had explained that even if they did, it was all organic. Earth to earth, nature to nature. Maeve had added that however tall oaks grew, their roots were rarely more than eighteen inches to two feet below ground as they spread across rather than down.

Now, with the soil trodden in, the interment was complete but the burial rite remained. Beth picked up a bowl full of early birch and oak leaves from nearby. She spread them in a wide circle around the new oak, enclosing it and themselves in a fairy ring of leaves instead of toadstools.

Maeve looked around her. In that short time, the sun had gone below the hill and the only light remaining was from the torches. Their flickering flames were turning the trees into something from a fairy tale - shadows, moving limbs, dark and light. Ruadhan stood again at the head of the grave, his arms raised in the air.

'Oh great gods of this earth, together we come to honour our sacred ancestor. Let us now weave our circle.'

Everyone held hands inside the leaf circle.

'Gather, spirits of sky, earth, fire and water and let this soul know that you bless him. Guide well his soul far beyond the realms of this world and into the next.

May this small oak grow to be a great oak, to stand and watch over him. Let him find calm and everlasting peace. So may it be.'

They bowed their heads in silence for a minute.

Michael then went over to fetch the crate of mead whilst Carole following on, laid the blankets out on the ground around the new Druid's Oak.

They had decided over dinner earlier that, as the lightning-struck oak had seen this farm through famine, witch-hunts and Puritanism; through restorations, wars and plagues, that it more than deserved the title of Druid's Oak. It was the only one that had been known around here for nearly five hundred years and was the focal point for the locals and their eagerly anticipated Pagan gatherings – whether they were church-goers or not!

The newly planted oak, therefore, was to be named Dallhain's Oak and as it was away from public places, could be kept as a fitting resting ground and a site of tranquility and solitude.

Carole had poured the mead, a generous serving because of the equally generous glasses. Incense had been lit in spills around the circle.

'Steady,' Beth said to Glenys. 'It's the homemade mead and it's a bit strong. Not like the stuff we normally have.'

Glenys waved this aside.

'It tastes like sweet cordial or maybe a honey-flavoured sherry. I'm sure I'll be fine; it doesn't taste very alcoholic.' Glenys knocked the mead back.

Beth looked doubtful and Maeve looked at Glenys and thought 'Who *is* this woman?'. Glenys had to have her glass refilled for the start of the normal Beltane ceremony.

Ruadhan held his glass up and they all followed suit. The torchlight sparkled through the glasses into the amber-coloured nectar. He started speaking.

'Hail Guardian Spirits. We welcome you to this Sacred Grove and ask that you accept our presence.

We come to celebrate Beltane and as the Tree of Life springs forth and Nature is renewed, we ask for your blessing.

As we gather here on this May Eve, let this fire guide us into the light and so may we have a spiritual awakening in our hearts.

May we have fruitfulness in our fields and peace, here in this place- and throughout the world.

Blessed Be.'

They all repeated 'Blessed Be' and then sat on the blankets to pass apples, bread, cheese and mead amongst themselves. Ruadhan produced his lyre harp from behind a tree.

'And for my next trick,' laughed Michael as Ruadhan did seem to be able to conjure things out of thin air when needed.

He played gentle songs then, as the mead flowed, more jaunty songs. Tunes they could dance to, so they did, all around the grove. Ruadhan said that, far from not respecting the dead, this was a joyous and time-honoured way of sending the departed on their journey to another life.

Later, Ruadhan drew Maeve aside. He had drunk far less than most people and spoke soberly.

'I can feel him Maeve. My ancestor is here with us – and he is happy.'

Maeve had to agree with him because she could feel it too.

CHAPTER 30

<u>May Day</u>

Maeve couldn't sleep. She had to pad downstairs in her pyjamas around five am. to make a cup of tea. She had only been asleep for a couple of hours altogether. It wasn't just the late night at Dallhain's Oak, it was something indefinable. As soon as she entered the kitchen, it became instantly definable. Michael was there, leaning back on a dining chair, a coffee in front of him. She jumped a little at his presence.

'Couldn't you sleep either?' she asked, filling a mug from the kettle simmering on the stove.

He didn't answer. She turned around to look at him. He was staring straight at her as though he could see inside her soul. She took a deep, shuddering breath.

'Neither could you?' he eventually asked. She lowered her eyes.

His coffee and her tea were left untouched as he grabbed her hand and headed towards the front door. Rusty just opened one sleepy eye and then shut it again, tolerant of the quirks of these humans.

'Where are we going?' she asked, not really caring as long as it was with Michael. His answer was to put his arm around her and kiss her head and then her ear, lingering to whisper to her.

They headed towards the clearing, then past it to the sacred pool. The sun was showing the same sultry promise of earlier days - the heat was there and promising much more for later. Rays of light were filtering down sparingly onto the still water. Only a mere trickle found its way down the rocks, making a pleasant, soothing sound, like a background to a meditation.

He pulled her towards the edge of the pool.

'Have you heard,' he said in a low voice, 'of the May Day morning traditions?'

She shook her head, not trusting herself to speak.

'With your bare feet, step into the dew, letting it caress your skin.'

She did this and he moved towards her.

'Then, we take off our clothes.'

As they were hardly wearing any in the first place, this took an indecently short time. Maeve's modesty seemed to have deserted her.

'Then,' his voice was husky and deep. 'We bind our wrists together and count to nine. If we are still together nine weeks hence, then we are together for life.'

He took a plaited leather cord that was wound around his wrist and bound both their wrists gently together. Then they looked into each other's eyes for nine seconds but it seemed to be forever. Maeve watched Michael's facial expression change from one of sincerity to one of adoration. Then to one of complete mischief.

'Then...' he said, taking off the cord and grasping her hand tightly. 'We–'

Any more words were lost as they plunged into the pool. It may have been the start of another glorious, red-hot day but the water was freezing!

Maeve gasped; her senses, as well as everything else, were numb. Michael laughed at her expression. He swam the short distance towards her and gathered her up to his bare chest. She put her head against it and then looked up at him. He kissed her deeply as he caressed her body and the clear water moved rhythmically around their bodies.

*

The trestle tables at the front of the farm were in imminent danger of collapsing under the weight of all the food. All the savoury food was here and everyone in the village was lined up, holding a plate in front of them in a passable imitation of Oliver Twist. Their friends from Helmsley were there too – the chemist, Mr Naughton at the hardware shop, the plantsman at Helmsley Walled Gardens, art suppliers, librarians – and everyone who had supported them.

Beth had given a short speech thanking everyone for their pledges and explaining why they wouldn't now be needed, even though the thought would always be remembered.

She directed them to the barn where there was a lot of ooh-ing and ah-ing at the gold objects and Kit and his wife Annie were on hand if anyone had any questions. The archaeology students had come to enjoy the celebration as well as their boss and even John Bradborough had made it here for the day. Maeve was disappointed that her parents couldn't come because of a previously arranged golf tournament in Spain but made them promise to come and meet everyone soon.

People were piling their plates up with delicious food. Fresh salmon or sliced chicken breast with six different types of salad. Pastries filled with chicken and mushroom or meat and potato, then herby cheese scones. Quiches of salmon and asparagus, ham and cheese, broccoli and cheese and leek and mushroom. There were Cornish pasties and pork and game pie. Crumbly sausage rolls filled the plates as well as spicy mashed potato patties. Dishes of potato salad and coleslaw were dotted at intervals as were plates of sliced savoury Beltane bread.

Maeve looked at the full plates and thought that there was no way on earth that people would be able to move on to the sweet stuff currently under clingfilm in the barn. She was surprised to see those who had been served first, already making a beeline for the barn. She was even more surprised after a relatively decent time gap to find herself making for it too. She picked up a clean plate.

There were strawberries and raspberries in huge bowls with cream in two others. There were apple and cinnamon fritters dusted with sugar and piles of fruit scones with plates of butter and strawberry jam nearby. Smaller plates of cream-filled brandy snaps filled up the spaces. Towards the back, there were slabs of honey cake, lavender cake and the traditional Beltane Bannock, made with eggs, milk, honey and oatmeal. An unusual addition, to Maeve anyway, was a sweet herb tart with basil, rosewater, vanilla and strawberries.

Carole had surpassed herself. They had all helped but she had worked day and night. She seemed to thrive on it and had even discussed a monthly supper club for the village to be held in the barn, to add extra to the money from the thriving market stall.

Beth was flitting between groups of people, greeting them as enthusiastically as they greeted her. She was determined to make a success of today to show her gratitude.

Maeve thought back to earlier this morning. She and Michael had tried to sneak back into the house, hair still streaming wet. Unfortunately, they bumped into Glenys in the hallway with a glass of water in one hand and a blister pack of painkillers in the other. She didn't seem to think there was anything strange about them coming in from outside at such an early hour. All she said was 'Don't ever mention mead to me again,' and then slowly made her way upstairs.

Michael had grinned from ear to ear.

'I'll never let her forget it.'

'Don't be awful,' said Maeve but had smiled all the same.

After a very early breakfast, Maeve had gathered the softer twigs full of leaves and flowers from shrubs around the grounds to weave into garlands for the resident's hair. Michael and Tim had predictably refused to wear them but were soon shamed into it by Ruadhan flaunting his garland and giving them reproachful looks. Even Rusty had a garland made for him which he tolerated quite well until it fell off and surprised him as he'd forgotten he was wearing it.

Maeve had made her garland as much like the one in the painting as she could. Instead of the white robe though, she was wearing her floaty floral frock. Michael had taken one look at her wearing the frock and the garland and his face softened.

'My May Queen,' he said, drawing her towards him for a kiss. They were both oblivious to Beth passing nearby and doing a little dance of triumph as she went around the corner.

Michael's painting was hung in the hallway on full display. Beth had been thrilled and wanted it hung here especially for May Day as that was what it represented.

Earlier, as people drifted into the grounds, Ruadhan had played an Elizabethan song – 'In a Glorious Garden Grene' - to the visitors in 'Maeve's' garden who wanted a peaceful start to the day in this oasis of calm. It would no doubt be used as such throughout the day.

The villagers had also 'brought in the May' and were wearing homemade garlands in their hair too. Mostly the women, it must be said but some of the more larger-than-life male stalwarts of The Falcon had embraced it, wearing enough flowers and foliage on their heads to start a florist's shop. On closer inspection, the various stuffed animals peeping out of their garlands weren't strictly part of the ritual but caused much hilarity amongst the children.

The food having been miraculously diminished and definitely enjoyed, Ruadhan took his lyre harp over to the Druid's Oak. The young girls in white robes and with garlanded hair, held hands around it. Other people gathered and formed a larger circle around the girls. Beth called Maeve over to join in. As Ruadhan played his tune – 'Now is the Month of Maying' – the girls danced round the oak one way while the outer circle danced in the other direction.

Michael, having mysteriously produced the bodhran and providing the beat, gave two loud raps on it whereupon everyone changed direction. This happened a few times until Ruadhan stopped playing and said 'It is time.'

A lovely girl of around eight years old with long curly hair and sparkling blue eyes, stepped forward, followed by two of the cutest little attendants, chubby hands holding posies of flowers.

Glenys carried a flower-covered crown and a green velvet cloak over and handed them with great ceremony to Beth, who thanked her. Then, as Ruadhan said 'We now declare you, Evie Roberts, to be our beautiful May Queen', Beth pulled the cloak around the girl's shoulders, placed the crown on her head and turned her to face her audience.

They all cheered loudly and then watched as the girl made a wide circle of the tree by herself this time, accompanied only by the two tiny little tots who were gazing around them in awe.

After this, the day became more informal and people did their own thing. The mead, ale and elderflower wine flowed freely. There was juice for the children and non-alcoholic elderflower water for the drivers as well as copious amounts of tea and coffee.

Maeve cringed as she watched Michael go over to where Glenys stood with Bert, Beth, Sam and his wife. He offered her a glass of mead and Glenys turned visibly green. Beth shook her head in despair but seemed amused all the same, especially when Michael put his arm around Glenys and gave her a hug, which made her recover somewhat.

Ruadhan and Michael played lyre and guitar while Sam joined in, showing his skill on the fiddle, playing tunes like 'Come Lasses and Lads' and 'Kemp's Jig'. Everyone whirled around on the grass, dancing their inhibitions away.

Michael had spread a couple of blankets beneath the Druid's Oak and the occupants of the farm took possession of it. They were all sitting there in the blessed shade when Ruadhan dashed over to them and took his place with eagerness.

'You'll never believe what Kit's just told me!'

Everyone looked at him waiting for his next words but Ruadhan stared back as though he expected an answer by extra-sensory perception. When he didn't get one, he went on.

'The British Museum who are having our 'Hawbury Hoard' as they are calling it...' he looked ridiculously pleased that it had a name, 'Have asked if they can publish *The Book of Dallhain*. They say it is the most important translation to emerge in recent years, especially as it is so closely associated with King Ceolwulf and the new finds.'

Everyone congratulated him sincerely. All his many years of hard work in even harder conditions had paid off at last. He was to be recognised as an expert in this field and especially on this period and area.

'I know you're not interested in money Ruadhan – but I hope they will be paying you?' asked Michael, practical as ever.

'They will – and from what Kit says, it will be a substantial amount. It depends on sales of course but it will be sold at their museum shop and on their website.'

'Perhaps…' Beth wavered a little here, almost afraid to voice her thoughts. 'Perhaps you would be able to do the tower up with the money?'

Ruadhan smiled gently at her, reading her thoughts.

'I would like to make it habitable Beth but the rest will go towards this place. I would use the tower as a workplace perhaps but more of the money needs to go into the farm and into our lifestyle. I have come to realise, since the storm, that no man is an island. I have come to appreciate the value of friendship, so I will still be living in the house if that's all right with you?'

Beth leant forward to tousle his hair.

'You know it is - with all of us,' and everyone agreed wholeheartedly.

Is Dr Ardley coming to join us?' Maeve asked. 'As he'll very soon be one of us.'

'He is, anytime now. Which reminds me. I was talking to a woman earlier. You may have seen me showing her round the far barn?'

Everyone looked clueless, apart from Maeve who had noticed Beth showing someone around the brick-built barn joined onto Tim's barn. The lady was a jolly-looking middle-aged lady, dressed in home-spun woollens even on a hot day. She had thick glasses on and a spiky, deep auburn haircut. She looked like a very smiley earth mother.

'Anyway, she likes the way we live here. She is very much into weaving and needs somewhere for her loom. She sells things at craft fairs and Viking festivals, as well as online. This 'set up' she says, is perfect for her. Space, nature, tranquillity and her sort of people. I wanted to say we are 'every type' of people you could possibly think of, not just one sort but she would find that out. Unfortunately, we haven't got any rooms for her at the moment but I took her name and phone number and said I'd let her know sometime in the future. What do you think?'

Everyone murmured their agreement that they would be happy for her to join them when the time came. Carole and Tim glanced across at each other, a secret look passing between them. Carole cleared her throat.

'Well actually, there might be rooms coming free,' she blushed.

'So,' Tim added. 'Go ahead and tell her there is space if you like. Carole is moving in with me.'

This macho display from Tim took them all so much by surprise that it took a minute to register. Then they all hugged them both happily. Michael earned an 'Oh dear' look from Beth as he said 'About time too' but she had to admit, it was a thought they all shared.

Beth also noticed the look that passed between Michael and Maeve when the announcement of moving in together had come. They smiled covertly and as Michael pulled Maeve towards him, she nestled up to him. Beth's heart felt full of hope. Of all the unresolved romances, this was one she particularly wanted to work. No one could predict how relationships were going to go but she had high expectations for this one.

She caught Maeve's eye and they regarded each other with affection. They had been on a long journey since that day on top of the cliffs, when they had first met.

Beth lifted her glass towards Maeve - and Maeve acknowledged this with a smile, raising her own glass. Maeve knew she was home and Beth was part of that home.

Beth then lifted her glass to everyone.

'A toast. To Druid's Oak Farm and to all my family. Here's to a successful and very happy future.'

Their cheers rang around the grounds and back up to the ancient oak, which looked down on the people and the land here, standing guard as it had always done.

Notes

Running an artistic retreat is something my daughter and I dream of – but for now, we will have to be content to use Druid's Oak Farm as our blueprint. As a fully restored farm, of course, with no leaky roof!

Druid's Oak Farm is completely imaginary but Hawbury is based very loosely on a village near to Helmsley.

Helmsley, along with its castle and walled garden, does exist. Rievaulx Abbey is a real place too and I urge you to visit both if you can.

I have tried to research Druids and Bards as closely as possible but the blessings and ceremonies are mostly imagined. The information regarding history, archaeology and trees is mostly researched and factual but I may have gone off at a tangent now and again if it helped the story. King Ceolwulf of Northumbria did exist and retired to Lindisfarne but he didn't have a bard named Dallhain – although you never know!

As usual in my books, Yorkshire and its wonderful countryside are the stars.

Printed in Great Britain
by Amazon